Quarto is the authority on a wide range of topics.

Quarto educates, entertains and enriches the lives of our readers—enthusiasts and lovers of hands-on living.

www.QuartoKnows.com

First published in the United States of America in 2016 by
Fair Winds Press, an imprint of
Quarto Publishing Group USA Inc.
100 Cummings Center
Suite 406-L
Beverly, Massachusetts 01915-6101
Telephone: (978) 282-9590
Fax: (978) 283-2742
QuartoKnows.com
Visit our blogs at QuartoKnows.com

20 19 18 17 16   1 2 3 4 5

ISBN: 978-1-59233-715-6
Digital edition published in 2016
eISBN: 978-1-62788-851-6
Library of Congress Cataloging-in-Publication Data available.

Design, cover, and page layout: Rita Sowins
Photography and cover image: Hayley Barisa Ryczek

Printed in China

The information in this book is for educational purposes only. It is not intended to replace the advice of a physician or medical practitioner. Please see your health-care provider before beginning any new health program.

fermented foods
foods
at *every meal*

Nourish Your Family at Every Meal with QUICK AND EASY
RECIPES USING THE TOP 10 LIVE-CULTURE FOODS

Hayley Barisa Ryczek

FAIR WINDS

Contents

Introduction

Whether or not you realize it, fermented foods are part of your everyday life. Fermentation is used in many of the foods you eat regularly, including salami, cheese, yogurt, prosciutto, and bread.

Fermentation has enjoyed a resurgence of interest in recent years, but it's actually been around for millennia. Every culture in the world has a distinctive history of fermentation, such as kimchi, natto, soy sauce, and fish sauce in Asia; crock-fermented sauerkraut and fermented fish in Northern Europe; and kefir and fermented pickles in the Middle East. Throughout the years, fermentation has been used to help preserve food, keeping it edible long after it was picked or caught fresh. In many ways, fermentation provided the first convenience foods, allowing food to be stored for long periods of time without refrigeration.

But what are fermented foods? Simply put, they are foods that have healthful microbes deliberately added to modify them. Though the bacteria that cause a winter's outbreak of strep throat are obviously harmful, not all bugs are bad. Bacteria can help keep us healthy in all kinds of ways—from bolstering our immune system to digesting food.

Oftentimes, whether bacteria are good or bad is a matter of balance. For example, candida is naturally occurring bacteria found in our bodies and in small amounts is benign. However, when stress, medications, and poor diet enable it to proliferate, it can seriously damage our intestinal lining and compromise our health in all sorts of ways. When a microbial system is in balance, good microbes keep the bad microbes in line. An overgrowth of bad microbes, however, can take over and disrupt the healthy balance.

Fermentation uses the good bacteria, commonly referred to as probiotics, to make food more nutritious. The fermentation process converts the starches in foods into something that's more easily digestible. Eating fermented foods introduces the living probiotic cultured microbes into our intestinal tracts and improves digestion, allowing us to absorb more nutrients in the foods we eat. We need these good microbes to keep a healthy balance after eating a diet rich in refined sugar and white flour foods and also to fight illness.

Unfortunately, the American food industry has a phobia when it comes to bacteria. In some ways, that's a good thing. Sterilization and pasteurization have saved many lives since becoming standard practice in the middle of the twentieth century, but a growing number of people argue that it's gone too far. The perceived threat of all bacteria in foods, good or bad, has led us to experience an imbalance of bacteria in our guts. This fear of bacteria is unfounded. In fact, historically people have survived *because* of good bacteria used to ferment foods and keep our digestive tracts healthy and running smoothly. By reintroducing traditional, fermented foods back into our diets, we can help to rebuild healthy gut bacteria.

In this book, I'll teach you all the reasons why you need to have fermented foods in your diet, how you can easily make 10 fermented foods that you and your family will love, and how to use those foods. Eating something fermented every day is a good starting point. From there, you can build up to integrating fermented foods into every meal. This can be as easy as eating yogurt with breakfast, fermented vegetables with lunch, and a fermented sauce with dinner. You can even squeeze in a refreshing glass of fizzy kombucha between meals! In these pages, you will find 100 recipes that will help you easily add fermented foods to every meal—and even times in between.

In health,

Hayley.

Chapter 1

The Benefits and Basics of *Fermenting Your Own Foods*

Imagine living to be 100 years old. Now imagine living to be 100 while retaining your vitality. You'd be in good company in Okinawa, an archipelago 360 miles off the coast of Japan. There, according to the *Okinawa Centenarian Study*, you'll find the world's highest prevalence of centenarians: 740 out of a population of 1.3 million. Okinawan seniors have not only the highest life expectancy in the world, but also the highest health expectancy. They have optimal health as they age, and don't experience as much age-related disease. Perhaps not coincidentally, these seniors consume traditionally fermented foods in the forms of miso, tofu, kimchi, and soy sauce as a regular part of their diets.

The number of studies showing the health benefits of eating a diet rich in fermented foods is growing. In particular, a 2006 study done by the Japanese Society of Allergology showed that fermented foods can lessen or reduce allergies as well as plaque in the mouth, which results in fewer cavities and healthier gums. The study also showed that many people even lose weight more easily when they include fermented foods in their diets.

When you make your own fermented foods, you will derive the greatest nutritional benefits from them. Commercially fermented products such as jarred pickles are no longer full of beneficial bacteria because they're simply cured in vinegar. The flavor, although similar, is rarely as robust as that of a traditional, homemade version. Even foods that are fermented using traditional methods can easily lose their health benefits when they are processed using pasteurization, which kills off all the beneficial bacteria that fermentation created!

FERMENTED FOODS FOR HEALTH

Including fermented foods regularly in your diet will provide many health benefits to your digestive system. Fermented foods improve digestion by supplying probiotic bacteria and restoring balance in your digestive tract. This is where the foods you eat are digested and all the nutrients are absorbed.

Bacterial balance in the digestive system is important for many reasons. When bad bacteria overcrowd your gut, that balance gets out of whack. Foodborne illness, commonly referred to as food poisoning, is one possibility. But other problems, including headaches, diarrhea, allergies, and even disease can result. Lifestyle habits are important to good overall health and many of our regular habits can influence our digestive health. Some bad habits including consumption of unhealthy, processed foods, stress, and even insufficient sleep can throw bacterial balance into a tailspin. Including fermented foods in your diet regularly is a good habit that can re-establish a healthy bacterial balance.

✳ *Prebiotics and Probiotics* ✳

Fermentation occurs because of the work of microbes. Microbes thrive on water and food, which are plentiful in the digestive tract. The probiotic microbes eat the foods we eat, and then create byproducts that change the texture and flavor of the foods. They consume sugars and produce carbon dioxide and alcohol. This can make foods a bit fizzy and sometimes sweet, tart, or savory. As they reach the intestinal tract, they spark the growth of even more probiotic microbes.

Fermented food labels often include the words "live" or "living." This is because the bacteria used to ferment foods are alive. In fact, the word probiotic is derived from the Greek word pro, which means "for" and bios, which means "life." Prebiotics are the carbohydrate-rich, non-digestible food source for probiotic microbes and they also create an environment in the digestive tract that allows them to survive and even thrive. Prebiotics are health promoting in other ways including lowering LDL, blood cholesterol, and triglyceride levels. Fermented foods typically include both the probiotic microbes and prebiotics.

When we have a bacterial infection, harmful bacteria have invaded our system to make us sick. We might be prescribed antibiotics to fight the illness or infection. The problem with antibiotics, however, is that they don't just kill the bad guys; they deplete the beneficial bacteria as well. Eating fermented foods can help boost our supply of healthful, probiotic bacteria which supports our immune system, establishes balance, and also fights off the bad guys.

✳ *Immune System Support* ✳

Our digestive tract is where all the magic happens to help us stay well. When we are fighting disease or illness, the bacterial balance in our gut is important to our immunity. In fact, the largest organ in our immune system is our gut, this is responsible for almost half of our immune response. Nearly 100 trillion bacteria populate our digestive tract. That's a heck of a lot of cells. It's hard to believe but because bacteria cells outweigh all other body cells, we are made up mostly of them.

When we think of neurotransmitters, we think of our brains. Indeed, our brains have plenty of them. But our gut also includes neurotransmitters and our gut actually includes as many neurotransmitters as our brain. Research shows that our gut is strongly connected to our immune system. The neurotransmitters in our gut communicate with our immune cells, activating and strengthening our immune system. For example, inflammation is thought to be connected to diseases such as arthritis, metabolic syndrome, and heart disease. The probiotic bacteria in fermented foods creates a healthful balance in our digestive tract, which can help the neurotransmitters connect with immune cells and impact healthy immunity and resistance to disease and illness.

✳ *Fermented Foods and Digestion* ✳

Keeping your digestive system healthy can help it do its job to break down foods and absorb nutrients and water. When you consume an unhealthy diet of processed foods, your digestive tract has to work hard to digest foods and absorb nutrients.

There are components of some of the foods we eat that can interfere with healthy digestion. Phylates are an example of one substance present in some foods that bind to nutrients, preventing them from being absorbed. Fermentation helps to remove substances such as phylates in foods to help your gut absorb nutrients properly.

Phylates, also known as phytic acid, store phosphorus in some of the foods we eat including seeds, nuts, legumes, and whole grains. They are concerning compounds since they bind to a portion of the iron, zinc, and calcium in foods, making these minerals unavailable for absorption.

Foods rich in phylates require some type of processing before we can even absorb nutrients from them. During certain food processes, enzymes called phytases destroy the phylates. These processes include the rising of yeast dough; the sprouting of seeds, grains, and legumes; the roasting of nuts; the presoaking of beans; the grinding of seeds; cooking; and fermentation.

When foods are fermented, they are actually partially digested. In yogurt production the probiotic bacteria digest milk sugar, or lactose, this can help people with lactose intolerance consume yogurt without digestive upset.

TIPS FOR BUYING FERMENTED FOODS

Although making fermented foods is very easy, there may be times when you don't have the time or energy to do so. If you want to occasionally supplement your homemade ferments with store-bought ones, I recommend going for local ferments when at all possible. Visit farmers' markets and neighborhood shops for ones that are produced locally and in smaller batches. These are likely to be better than big national brands. And be careful—it's easy to buy things that sound fermented but are not, like many kinds of sauerkraut and pickles. Live fermented foods in a supermarket will always be in the refrigerator section and have words like "raw," "unpasteurized," "live," "active," and "cultures" on their labels. If it's not refrigerated, either it's not live or it's not fermented.

AN OVERVIEW OF FERMENTATION

Historically, there is evidence that fermentation has been used in cultures living in Asia, South America, and Europe. Early use of fermentation involved some trial and error, testing of various temperatures, addition of sugar or salt, and timing. This experimentation of methods was critical to not only maintaining a fresh food supply, but also creating processes that greatly helped in improving flavor and healthfulness of foods.

Fermentation involves creating a living ecosystem with several different organisms working in unison to thrive. We have a good understanding today of how this ecosystem works. Different species of bacteria are used in the process and the types of bacteria that form determine whether the outcome is successful.

The bacteria used in fermentation contain different properties, survive on different types of nutrition, and compete for the nutrients available. The fermented foods will look, feel, and taste a certain way (as is the case of *Kombucha Soda*, page 100) based on the properties of the bacteria. The requirements for controlled fermentation, then, are a desirable strain of microbes, the right type of organic material, and the ability to create the optimum environment for fermentation.

✳ *The Process of Fermentation* ✳

Sometimes foods are fermented by organisms in the environment. These organisms are not selected or added to the foods but occur naturally in the environment surrounding the food. The organisms include wild yeasts and other strains of bacteria found in the atmosphere. This is called uncontrolled fermentation. Sometimes this process works and is beneficial for the food and sometimes this process spoils the food. Over time, when refrigeration was not available, people learned to control this process to preserve drinks and foods.

Fungi and bacteria are two types of organisms that participate in fermentation. When fermenting alcohol, fungi are used, and bacteria in fermentation produce acids. In some cases, they are used together.

When cheese, wine, sourdough bread, and beer are fermented, fungi or yeasts are used in this process. Yeasts produce ethanol and during fermentation ethanol produces carbon dioxide (creating spaces or holes in a light, fluffy loaf of sourdough bread). Sometimes fermentation yields surprising results. In this case, producing alcohol is not the goal of using yeasts, but the alcohol nevertheless imparts a satisfying flavor.

The tangy flavor of foods can be attributed to *Lactobacillus* bacteria, which produces lactic acid. This type of bacteria is used in the fermentation of sausages, vegetables, and cheese. *Lactobacillus* is one of the most common types of bacteria used in fermentation. *Acetobacter*, which is another strain of bacteria that produces acetic acid, is used in wine and hard cider.

✳ *Introducing a Desirable Strain of Bacterial Growth in the Perfect Environment* ✳

Sometimes fermentation is used for making bread or pickling vegetables. The yeast that occurs in the wild and is present on foods as well as the bacteria on the foods promotes an environment for wild fermentation.

Bacteria present in cultures or starters are also used in fermentation. This process involves using probiotic bacteria to produce lactic acid (this method is used to make pickles with a tart flavor). During this process, bacteria that may promote mold and spoiling of the foods are destroyed.

Various types of bacteria are used during fermentation, and each type requires a certain type of environment. Certain strains of bacteria cannot survive when exposed to oxygen (anaerobic strains) while other types need lots of oxygen (aerobic strains). Some types prefer a very warm environment (thermophilic), others require a very cold environment (cryophilic), and still others prefer moderate temperatures (hemophilic).

The anaerobic fermentation process used to ferment some fruits, vegetables, dairy, and meat is called lacto-fermentation. This process works by inhibiting oxygen use by bacteria that typically cause rot, thereby creating an environment where good bacteria flourish. During this process, lactic acid is produced lending a distinctive flavor to the foods. This process also helps make yogurt from milk.

Some types of fermentation use salt. Salt acts to reduce the availability of water during the fermentation process. It also changes the pH or acid level of the food and creates an environment in which certain types of bacteria (such as *Lactobacillus*) flourish.

Other types of bacteria cause food spoilage. Some types compete with good, probiotic bacteria, thereby preventing fermentation. A successful fermentation process would include the probiotic bacteria surviving and promoting a tasty, tart yogurt or tangy sauerkraut from the cabbage, while prohibiting the bad bacteria to flourish and overwhelm the process causing spoiled sauerkraut or yogurt. Once this process is perfected, the same process can be used the next time yogurt or sauerkraut are produced for consistency in both taste and texture of the food.

FERMENTING FOODS AT HOME

You can ferment almost any food as long as you have the right combination of microbes and nourishment, as well as a few supplies and ingredients on hand. The basic ingredients for fermentation aren't exotic or difficult to find; in fact, you probably have most of them in your kitchen right now. For help finding any supplies, cultures, or starters referenced in this book, turn to the resources on page 184 for my recommendations.

 THE DIFFERENCE BETWEEN FERMENTATION AND SPOILING

Safety is a major concern for lacto-fermented foods. But fermented foods are far more likely to resist spoilage than other foods because their environment is unfriendly to those types of microbes. Fermented foods can spoil, of course, but when they do, your eyes and nose are a sufficient warning system.

The process of fermentation is complex and involves many variables. Regardless of how many interlocking systems there may be at work, at a cellular level, the cook's work when it comes to creating fermented foods is direct and straightforward; the waiting is probably the hardest part.

✻ *Start with the Best Base* ✻

By starting with best-quality foods, you are taking the easiest first step toward ensuring a successful fermentation. And by choosing organic, you're ensuring your foods aren't exposed to pesticides or other harmful chemicals that could stand in the way of the fermentation process.

Fresh produce: Always use the freshest and best-quality ingredients, preferably organic. Fermentation has traditionally been used to preserve foods that are seasonally fresh. As a general rule, rinse and trim fruits and vegetables to remove stems or bruises.

Salt: The type of salt you use can make a difference in the way your ferments taste. It's a matter of personal preference, but I do not recommend using iodized table salt since it contains iodine, dextrose (sugar), and anticaking ingredients, all of which can affect the taste and appearance of your ferments. I use only Celtic sea salt or Himalayan salt in my recipes.

Water: If your drinking water is treated with chlorine or fluoride, it is advisable to use filtered or bottled spring water for fermentation.

Dairy: Raw milk, where available, is the best option for fermentation. If raw milk is not available, however, use any milk or cream that is not ultra-pasteurized or treated with preservatives for the recipes in this book.

For the Kefir, Yogurt, and Crème Fraîche, you have the option to use nondairy milk alternatives in conjunction with a specific starter designed to culture nondairy milks. It's important to choose brands made with no thickeners or additives.

Starters, cultures, kefir grains, and SCOBY: Some of the recipes in this book, such as Kefir and Kombucha, require starter grains and SCOBYs (symbiotic culture of bacteria and yeasts). Refer to the resources on page 184.

✳ *Basic Supplies and Equipment* ✳

You can make many of these fermented foods using ingredients that you have on hand or can get easily (and cheaply) at a hardware or grocery store. We have refined the techniques of fermentation over time. There are a variety of tools used in the fermentation process—ranging from using one's senses to judge color, flavor, or texture to more accurate tools such as thermometers, hydrometers, metering tubes, and siphons. But here's a basic list of items that may be useful when you're starting out:

- » Measuring cups
- » Measuring spoons
- » Fine-mesh strainer
- » Cheesecloth or cotton fabric
- » Rubber bands or string
- » Bowls
- » Knives
- » Wooden pounders or tampers
- » Graters or food processor with grating blade

- » Mandoline
- » Cutting board
- » Vegetable peeler
- » Funnel
- » Various-size wide-mouth glass canning jars with airtight lids
- » Bottles and caps for fermented beverages
- » Weights or airlocks

 THE IMPORTANCE OF SANITATION

Cleanliness matters. Always thoroughly wash all of your tools and containers in hot, soapy water. Use a bottlebrush to reach inside containers and make sure that you clean out any crevices or corners completely. Rinse everything in hot water. Clean your hands and cutting boards as well. There is no need to sterilize or use any chemicals—just follow basic, thorough hygiene.

✳ *Controlling the Temperature* ✳

Depending on the type of fermented food you are making, you will need to create an environment that will encourage the growth of healthy bacteria. The recipes in this book are primarily done at room temperature (roughly 68°F, or 20°C). Some recipes, however, such as Yogurt (page 166), require a warmer environment, between 90° and 125°F (32° and 52°C). I will always specify when a warmer temperature is necessary.

If your home is colder than 68°F (20°C), like ours in the winter, you can set up an inexpensive warm fermentation area by using a heated seed-starting mat to raise the temperature of your ferments. The addition of a thermostat will give you even greater control. See the resources (page 185) for my recommendations.

 DO'S AND DON'TS OF FERMENTATION

» Keep ferments out of direct sunlight.
» Avoid moving or jiggling foods while fermenting.
» If your ferments attract fruit flies, place a small glass filled with ½ inch (1.3 cm) of apple cider vinegar and a drop of dish soap nearby. It will attract them, and when they land on the liquid, the detergent will make them stick.

Chapter 2

Crème *Fraîche*

Crème fraîche is a skinny version of sour cream. Used as a topping, in sauces, or in a variety of savory or sweet uses, it has a delightful tanginess that comes from bacterial cultures.

There are several different methods for making crème fraîche. When crème fraîche is made in the United States, the processing of cream and most dairy ingredients requires pasteurization. This process removes bacteria, so fermentation is used to culture the bacteria. The unpasteurized or raw cream available in France contains bacteria, and when this cream is left out at room temperature during the aging process, the bacteria form a culture.

Beneficial bacteria, in the form of cultured buttermilk or a starter, are introduced into cream, transforming it into crème fraîche. During fermentation, the lactic acid bacterium, *Lactococcus lactis*, is added to the cream and these bacteria use the milk sugar, lactose, to become lactic acid. This lactic acid formation raises the pH level of the product. This increase in pH level also changes the flavor and inhibits the formation of bad bacteria in the product.

It's very easy to make crème fraîche with pasteurized cream. Simply combine buttermilk with heavy cream and then leave it at room temperature for half a day. Though this may seem like an unsafe practice, the bacteria present actually keep it from spoiling. Once made, the crème fraîche can be used in dressings, dips, and even ice cream! (Keep in mind, however, that heating it to higher than 100°F [(38°C)] will kill most of the beneficial bacteria.)

Crème Fraîche

YIELD: 2 CUPS (460 G)

- -

EQUIPMENT YOU'LL NEED:

*1 glass pint jar (475 ml)
with lid*

Mixing spoon

*Cheesecloth or cotton
fabric square*

Rubber band or string

INGREDIENTS:

*2 cups (475 ml) heavy or
whipping cream*

*2 tablespoons (28 ml)
cultured buttermilk or
packaged starter
(See Note on page 21.)*

Crème fraîche is pretty easy to make, and that's a good thing, because it can be hard to find in the store. It's a bit nutty and buttery tasting, and it can be used as a substitute for mayonnaise, yogurt, or sour cream in your favorite dish. It can also be used sweetened and whipped. Or you can whip it up (unsweetened) until it separates into solid butter and liquid buttermilk (which is different from the cultured buttermilk used in this recipe).

- -

Place the cream and buttermilk in a jar with a lid. Cover securely and shake for 15 seconds. Remove the lid and cover with the cheesecloth, securing with a rubber band or string. Set aside at room temperature for 12 to 24 hours until thickened similar to sour cream. (This time frame will avary depending on the cream and the temperature of your home.)

Stir the thickened crème fraîche well. Replace the lid tightly and refrigerate for at least 6 hours before serving. It will become even thicker as it chills. Store in the refrigerator for up to 2 weeks.

NOTES: Although it is generally recommended to avoid the use of ultra-pasteurized dairy products for culturing, I have found through many test batches that ultra-pasteurized cream works as well as all other types of cream in making Crème Fraîche.

If using a packaged crème fraîche starter, follow the instructions provided with the starter. See the resources (page 184) for where to buy.

 BUTTERMILK

Cultured buttermilk, available in the dairy section of any grocery store, differs from old-fashioned buttermilk, which is not cultured. Because of their significant differences in taste and texture, the two cannot be used interchangeably.

In recipes calling for old-fashioned buttermilk, you can substitute water with a small amount of lemon juice added (1 cup [235 ml] water to 1 tablespoon [15 ml] lemon juice). Replace cultured buttermilk by mixing sour cream or plain yogurt with a bit of water to achieve the right consistency and use it as you would buttermilk.

To Make Cultured Buttermilk: Using either a buttermilk starter or leftover buttermilk, in a 1-to-16 ratio of buttermilk to milk, mix the two together and pour into a glass jar. Cover the jar with a coffee filter or cheesecloth but do not seal it with a lid. Leave at room temperature, between 70° and 78°F (21° and 26°C), for 10 to 24 hours. When the milk moves away from the sides of the jar as a single mass, the buttermilk is ready. Seal the jar and refrigerate for 6 hours. Stir before using.

Western Omelet with Avocado Crème

YIELD: 4 SERVINGS

FOR THE AVOCADO CRÈME:

1 large ripe avocado

½ cup (115 g) Crème Fraîche (See page 20.)

Juice of 1 lime

Sea salt and ground black pepper, to taste

FOR THE OMELETS:

12 large eggs, divided

Sea salt and ground black pepper, to taste

4 tablespoons (55 g) butter, divided

½ of a green bell pepper, finely chopped

½ of a red bell pepper, finely chopped

6 ounces (170 g) cooked ham, finely chopped

4 scallions (white and green parts), finely chopped

½ cup (58 g) grated cheese, such as Monterey Jack, Cheddar, or Gouda (optional)

The creamy texture of this omelet comes from the melted cheddar and Monterey Jack cheeses. The colorful, crisp veggies folded inside lend a decadent flavor to this classic egg dish. For a probiotic treat, it's topped with delicious Avocado Crème.

MAKE THE AVOCADO CRÈME: Slice the avocado in half and remove the pit. Scoop the flesh into a food processor and add the Crème Fraîche, lime juice, and a big pinch of salt and pepper. Blend until smooth, cover, and chill in the refrigerator until ready to serve.

MAKE THE OMELET: In a small bowl, beat together 3 of the eggs and season lightly with salt and pepper. Set aside.

Heat 3 tablespoons (42 g) of the butter in a small nonstick skillet with a tight-fitting lid over medium heat. Add the bell peppers and cook, covered, without stirring, until tender, about 3 minutes. Uncover and raise the heat to medium-high. Add the ham and scallions and cook, stirring frequently, until hot, about 1 minute. Transfer the mixture to a bowl.

Melt a nut-size piece of the remaining 1 tablespoon (14 g) butter in the skillet over medium heat. When the foam subsides, add one-quarter of the pepper mixture. Pour in the beaten eggs and cook, stirring constantly with a heat-resistant rubber spatula, until just cooked, about 30 seconds. Turn off the heat and, using the rubber spatula, smooth the top of the omelet so that it evenly covers the inside of the skillet. Sprinkle about 2 tablespoons (7 g) of the cheese, if using, over the omelet. Let rest for 30 seconds or until the omelet has set.

Using the rubber spatula, fold the omelet in half and transfer to a warmed plate. Cover with aluminum foil to keep warm. Repeat with the remaining ingredients to make 3 more omelets. Top with the Avocado Crème.

Classic Chopped Salad with Green Goddess Dressing

The Cobb salad is a staple at many fine restaurants. This is a terrific one-dish meal filled with protein-rich eggs, bacon, and cheese, as well as crisp veggies. It's made special with a delicious, herbal, and probiotic-rich dressing.

FOR THE DRESSING:

1 cup (40 g) loosely packed fresh basil

½ cup (115 g) Crème Fraîche (See page 20.)

⅓ cup (20 g) loosely packed fresh flat-leaf parsley

2 tablespoons (28 ml) olive oil

2 tablespoons (28 ml) freshly squeezed lemon juice

2 cloves of garlic, minced

Sea salt and ground black pepper, to taste

MAKE THE DRESSING: Place the basil, Crème Fraîche, parsley, olive oil, lemon juice, garlic, and salt and pepper in a blender. Blend until smooth and refrigerate until ready to serve.

MAKE THE SALAD: Divide the salad greens among 4 plates. Layer with the chicken, tomatoes, avocado, eggs, bacon, and cheese. Top with the Green Goddess Dressing right before serving.

FOR THE SALAD:

5 cups (275 g) mixed spring greens

2 cups (280 g) chopped or shredded cooked chicken

2 cups (360 g) grape tomatoes, halved

1 ripe avocado, pitted, peeled, and diced

4 hard-boiled eggs, peeled and chopped

4 slices of bacon, cooked and crumbled

2 ounces (55 g) feta cheese or blue cheese, crumbled

Probiotic Creamy Ranch Dressing and Dip

YIELD: 2 CUPS (475 G)

----

1 cup (225 g) Fermented
    Mayonnaise (See
    page 156.)

1 cup (230 g) Crème
    Fraîche (See page 20.)

2 teaspoons dried parsley

2 teaspoons dried chives

1 teaspoon raw apple
    cider vinegar

1 teaspoon garlic powder

1 teaspoon onion powder

½ teaspoon sea salt

¼ teaspoon ground
    black pepper

Ranch is one of the most popular salad dressings and veggie dips. By simply making it with cultured Crème Fraîche, you can easily sneak a healthy dose of probiotics into many of your meals. And trust me, this tastes so much better than any version you can buy. One bite and you'll be hooked!

In a bowl, combine the Fermented Mayonnaise, Crème Fraîche, parsley, chives, vinegar, garlic powder, onion powder, sea salt, and pepper. Mix well. Store in the refrigerator for up to 1 week.

NOTE: Add milk, 1 tablespoon (at a time, if needed to thin to the 15 ml) desired consistency.

Herbed Seafood Salad

YIELD: 4 SERVINGS

- 8 ounces (225 g) cooked and peeled wild-caught shrimp
- 8 ounces (225 g) imitation crab
- ⅓ cup (77 g) Crème Fraîche (See page 20.)
- ⅓ cup (75 g) Fermented Mayonnaise (See page 156.)
- ½ teaspoon dried dill weed
- ½ teaspoon dried parsley
- Juice of ½ of a lemon
- Sea salt and ground black pepper, to taste

I've been making this seafood salad for years, as it's one of my husband's favorite cold salads. It's my re-creation of a popular deli salad, hence the inclusion of imitation crab, or surimi. If you prefer, you can substitute lump crabmeat. Serve this as a sandwich, on top of salad greens, or—our favorite way—right out of the bowl with a fork.

Coarsely chop the shrimp and shred the crab. Combine both in a large bowl.

In a separate bowl, combine the Crème Fraîche, Fermented Mayonnaise, dill, parsley, lemon juice, salt, and pepper. Mix well.

Toss the dressing with the seafood. Refrigerate, covered, for at least 1 hour prior to serving.

Cheesy Beef Stuffed Baked Potatoes

YIELD: 4 SERVINGS

- -

4 medium russet potatoes

1 pound (455 g) ground beef

½ of a green bell pepper, chopped

½ of a small red onion, chopped

1 can (15 ounces, or 425 g) of tomato sauce

2 tablespoons (32 g) tomato paste

1 tablespoon (15 ml) Worcestershire sauce

1½ teaspoons chili powder

¼ teaspoon ground black pepper

½ cup (58 g) shredded Cheddar cheese

½ cup (115 g) Crème Fraîche (See page 20.)

Chopped fresh chives or scallions, for garnish

Serving chessy beef filling in a baked potato is the perfect way to take something ordinary and make it extraordinary! It's family friendly and, when served with a healthy dollop of Crème Fraîche, is a stealthy way to get a fermented food into your meal if you are serving this to your kids.

- -

Preheat the oven to 400°F (200°C, or gas mark 6). Line a baking sheet with a silicone baking mat or parchment paper.

Use a fork to poke several holes in each potato. Bake the potatoes on the baking sheet until tender, about 45 minutes.

Meanwhile, heat a large skillet over medium-high heat. Add the ground beef, bell pepper, and onion. Cook for 8 to 10 minutes until the beef is cooked through, breaking up the beef with the side of a spoon. Reduce the heat to medium and add the tomato sauce, tomato paste, Worcestershire sauce, chili powder, and black pepper. Simmer for 3 to 5 minutes until thickened.

Slice off a small portion from the top of each potato. Use a small spoon to scoop out some of the potato flesh. Spoon the sloppy Joe mixture into the potatoes, top with the cheese and Crème Fraîche, and garnish with the chives or scallions.

✳ WHY PASTURE-RAISED BEEF IS BEST

Many people don't realize that grass—not corn, soy, or other grains—is the natural diet of cows. So it only makes sense that we should want to get beef from cows that have lived on pasture, rather than from those that were raised on genetically modified grain and soy, chock-full of growth hormones, steroids, and antibiotics. In addition:

» It is naturally higher in healthy fats proven and lower in bad fats.
» It contains seven times the amount of healthy omega-3 fatty acids as grain-fed beef.
» It has the recommended ratio of omega-3 to omega-6 fats.
» It is packed with minerals, vitamins, and conjugated linoleic acid (CLA), which has been linked to a reduced risk of cancer, diabetes, obesity, and various immune disorders.

Find local sources for grass-fed beef at www.eatwild.com and www.localharvest.org.

Grilled Peaches with Honey Crème and Granola Crumble

YIELD: 4 SERVINGS

FOR THE GRANOLA CRUMBLE:

½ cup (14 g) pumpkin seeds

½ cup (50 g) walnuts

½ cup (73 g) almonds

½ cup (50 g) pecans

½ cup (68 g) hazelnuts

3 tablespoons (60 g) maple syrup

2 tablespoons (28 g) coconut oil, melted

1 teaspoon ground cinnamon

½ teaspoon sea salt

FOR THE HONEY CRÈME:

1 cup (230 g) Crème Fraîche (See page 20.)

2 tablespoons (40 g) raw honey

FOR THE GRILLED PEACHES:

4 ripe peaches, halved and pitted

This dessert has a range of textures and flavors to satisfy everyone on a hot summer night.

Preheat the oven to 300°F (150°C, or gas mark 2). Line a baking sheet with parchment paper or grease well with coconut oil.

MAKE THE GRANOLA CRUMBLE: In a food processor, combine the pumpkin seeds, walnuts, almonds, pecans, and hazelnuts. Pulse until coarsely broken into small bits, but do not overprocess.You want a chunky, granola-size crumble. Transfer to a large bowl and set aside.

In a small bowl, mix the maple syrup, coconut oil, cinnamon, and salt. Pour onto the ground nut-seed mixture and stir until combined.

Evenly spread the mixture over the prepared baking sheet with the back of a spoon.

Bake for 10 minutes, continually checking and stirring to ensure even browning. Be careful not to burn. After the nuts and seeds are toasted and browned, set aside to cool completely.

Take a wooden spoon or spatula and break apart the mixture into smaller pieces, resembling granola. Store in an airtight Mason jar at room temperature for later use. (See Note below.)

MAKE THE HONEY CRÈME: In a small bowl, mix together the Crème Fraîche and honey until well blended. Refrigerate until ready to use.

MAKE THE GRILLED PEACHES: Preheat your grill or grill pan to medium-high and place the peaches cut side down. (You may want to add a bit of coconut oil to the surface of the grill to prevent them from sticking.) Grill for about 10 minutes or until tender.

Transfer the peaches to a platter or individual bowls. Spoon 1 to 2 tablespoons (15 to 28 g) of the Honey Crème on top of each half (grill mark side up). Garnish by sprinkling the tops with the Granola Crumbled. Serve immediately.

NOTE: Without the Honey Crème, the granola makes about 2½ cups (340 g). Enjoy leftovers as a topping to Yogurt (see page 166) and fresh fruit or as a bowl of cereal with cold milk.

Berry-Topped Chèvre Cheesecake Cups

YIELD: 6 SERVINGS

- -

1 teaspoon powdered
   gelatin

1 cup (235 ml) heavy
   cream, divided

8 ounces (225 g) chèvre
   (goat cheese)

½ cup (115 g) Crème
   Fraîche (See page 20.)

2 tablespoons (40 g) raw
   honey, plus more for
   drizzling

2 cups (290 g) fresh
   strawberries, hulled
   and chopped

Fresh mint, for garnish

The only thing better than cheesecake is one that's no-bake and full of healthy probiotics. But don't worry. No one needs to know how easy and healthy these delicious cheesecake cups are!

- -

Place the gelatin in a saucepan with 2 to 3 tablespoons (28 to 45 ml) of the cream and gently heat over medium-low heat to melt the gelatin. Set aside to cool slightly.

In a separate bowl, whisk together the chèvre, Crème Fraîche, and honey until smooth.

In another bowl, whisk or beat the remaining cream until stiff peaks form. Using a spatula, fold the cooled gelatin mixture into the goat cheese mixture and then fold in the whipped cream until fully combined.

Divide the mixture among six half-pint (235 ml) jelly jars. Cover and chill for at least 1 hour. Top each cheesecake cup with chopped strawberries, a drizzle of honey, and mint.

Cherry Compote Ice Cream

YIELD: 4 TO 6 SERVINGS

FOR THE CHERRY COMPOTE:

2 cups (310 g) pitted
 black cherries (fresh
 or frozen)
½ cup (100 g) sugar
Juice of ½ of a lemon

FOR THE ICE CREAM:

½ cup (100 g) sugar
6 egg yolks
¾ cup (175 ml) whole milk
2 cups (460 g) Crème
 Fraîche (See page 20.)

The buttery ice cream in this recipe is mixed with tart cherry compote for a truly dreamy dessert and a surprising mixture of textures to tantalize your tongue. Impress your family and friends with this four-star-restaurant–worthy offering that will have everyone begging you for the recipe.

MAKE THE CHERRY COMPOTE: Combine the cherries, sugar, and lemon juice in a small saucepan over low heat. Cook until the mixture looks like jam, about 20 minutes, stirring frequently.

Remove from the heat and allow to cool completely before layering with the ice cream.

MAKE THE ICE CREAM: In a bowl, whisk together the sugar and egg yolks until light and creamy.

In a medium saucepan over medium-low heat, heat the milk just until a few bubbles start to form. Slowly and gradually, pour the hot milk over the sugar and yolk mixture, whisking constantly. Transfer the mixture to the refrigerator for 6 hours or until completely chilled.

Using a blender or electric mixer, combine the chilled mixture and the Crème Fraîche until smooth.

Churn the mixture in an ice cream machine according to the manufacturer's directions. Once churned, scoop a few spoonfuls of the ice cream into a container and then add a few spoonfuls of the Cherry Compote. Continue layering and then cover with a lid or plastic wrap and store in the freezer until ready to serve or for up to 1 month.

NOTE: You can use strawberries in place of the cherries. You can also layer the mango syrup from the Sweet Mango Chutney Sundaes (page 65) in place of the berries, if desired.

Pavlova with Berries and Cream

YIELD: ONE 8- OR 9-INCH
(20 OR 23 CM) CAKE OR 6
INDIVIDUAL CAKES

- -

3 large egg whites

*½ cup (100 g) granulated
sugar*

*¼ cup (30 g)
confectioners' sugar*

*1¼ cups (290 g) Crème
Fraîche (See page 20.)*

*4 cups (approximately
580 g) fresh
berries (You can
use raspberries,
blueberries,
strawberries, or your
favorites.)*

Pavlova is traditionally topped with fresh berries or cut fruit and
whipped cream. It's made from meringue that is baked until it's
hardened on the outside, yet still tender and chewy on the inside.
The result is unique and a real treat! You may want to make six
small cakes or one large cake with this mixture. You'll notice
some cracks and dips in the cake's surface. This is to be expected
and is part of the natural beauty of this dessert.

- -

Preheat the oven to 200°F (95°C) and line a baking sheet with
parchment paper.

In the bowl of an electric mixer, beat the egg whites on medium-
high speed. When the egg whites form soft peaks, slowly add the
granulated sugar. Beat on high speed until stiff peaks form. Gently
fold in the confectioners' sugar with a spatula.

Spoon the meringue onto the parchment paper as one large pavlova or 6 equal-size smaller mounds. Smooth the top(s) and make a
slight indent in the center. Bake for about 2 hours or until the surface
of the meringue appears hard and dry. Cool completely.

Top the cooled pavlova with Crème Fraîche and fresh berries.
Serve immediately.

NOTE: Avoid making pavlova on humid days. The sugar in the delicate
egg white mixture readily absorbs moisture from the air, which makes
it soft and impossible to achieve thick, stiff peaks.

Chapter 3

Kefir

You may have seen kefir (keh-FEAR) in your dairy aisle and wondered about it. It's a drink with a thin, yogurt-like consistency, made from milk culture particles called grains. These are jelly-like particles that are white or yellow, and they are made from a yeast and probiotic bacteria mixture combined with a milk protein called casein. The grains can range in size from a tiny piece of dry couscous to the size of a kidney bean, and this size variation is completely normal. Grains ferment in the milk product to add probiotic bacteria.

Kefir is the gold standard of the healthful powers of probiotic bacteria. The kefir grains are packed with many different types of probiotic bacteria. Typically, about 50 strains of bacteria are found in kefir, which is amazing because each strain imparts unique health benefits. As a comparison, standard yogurt typically includes two strains of bacteria, unless the label states otherwise.

Kefir has many health benefits. For example, it:

» is good for digestion

» balances bacteria in your gut by populating good bacteria and reducing the amount of bad bacteria

» supplies calcium, magnesium, and other minerals to help stabilize blood pressure

» supplies tryptophan, an essential amino acid that is important for proper functioning of the nervous system and can help with conditions such as depression and sleep problems

» is tolerated well by people with lactose intolerance because the bacteria predigests the lactose (milk sugars) in the milk.

Kefir

EQUIPMENT YOU'LL NEED:

2 glass quart (950 ml)
    jars with lids
Wooden mixing spoon
Cheesecloth or cotton
    fabric square
Rubber band or string
Fine-mesh strainer

INGREDIENTS:

¼ cup (60 g) kefir grains
4 cups (950 ml) milk

Kefir has a tart and tangy taste. The fermentation time determines the flavor and thickness. You may even achieve a bubbly or fizzy result. This is a versatile recipe drink Kefir as a beverage or add it to smoothies. Kefir has been around for centuries and was thought to possibly have been created by accident. If so, it was a healthful and tasty accident!

Add the kefir grains and milk to a glass jar. Stir gently using a wooden spoon.

Cover the jar with cheesecloth secured with a rubber band or string and allow to ferment at room temperature (out of direct sunlight) for 12 to 48 hours.

You can taste the kefir to see whether it has properly fermented, or watch for the whey (a clear yellowish liquid) to separate at the bottom of the jar. You may have small pockets of whey throughout the kefir.

Pour the kefir through a small fine-mesh strainer into another clean jar, collecting the kefir grains in the strainer for use in another batch. (See "Caring for Kefir Grains" on page 37.)

Chill the kefir, covered, for the best taste results. You can drink it plain, although many people sweeten it with a bit of maple syrup or honey or blend it with fresh fruit. Store in the refrigerator for up to 2 weeks.

NOTE: You can purchase kefir grains (see resources on page 184), but most often, they are shared among friends.

✳ CARING FOR KEFIR GRAINS

Kefir will ferment slower in a cool environment and quicker in a warm room. If you want your Kefir to have a thick consistency, allow it to culture for longer. If you have kefir grains and you're not ready to ferment a new batch, store them in the refrigerator covered with milk. They will enter a dormant state. When you're ready to ferment a batch using the refrigerated grains, the process will take a bit more time.

If you're starting a new batch of Kefir using grains from a previous batch, it's not necessary to rinse the grains. When a little bit of the last batch of Kefir clings to the grains, this keeps them strong and hardy. If you drop your grains on the floor, the kitchen counter, or in the sink, or add the wrong type of milk, rinse them promptly to remove potentially harmful bacteria. When rinsing grains, always use fresh spring water or distilled water because tap water contains minerals that can interfere with the fermentation process.

Chocolate Peanut Butter Banana Breakfast Smoothie

YIELD: 2 (1¼-CUPS, OR 285 ML) SERVINGS

- -

1 cup (235 ml) milk

1 banana, cut into chunks

¼ cup (60 ml) Kefir (See page 36.)

2 tablespoons (32 g) peanut butter

1 tablespoon (5 g) unsweetened cocoa powder

1 tablespoon (20 g) raw honey

1 cup (118 g) ice cubes

It would be so nice to have a hot breakfast every day. Eggs, bacon, hash browns—the works. But it's time-consuming to prepare, not to mention the cleanup. Instead, you can have a complete, filling, nourishing breakfast with this smoothie. Toss the ingredients into a blender, pour into a to-go container, and be on your way! If you need a little boost, you can even throw in a bit of espresso powder. This easy-to-prepare breakfast will have you hooked.

- -

In a blender, combine the milk, banana, Kefir, peanut butter, cocoa powder, honey, and ice cubes and blend until smooth. Serve immediately.

VARIATIONS
Use any other nut or seed butter in place of the peanut butter.
Use stevia or maple syrup in place of the honey.

Butter Lettuce Salad with Gorgonzola Pear Dressing

YIELD: 4 SERVINGS

- -

FOR THE DRESSING:

⅓ cup (80 ml) extra-virgin olive oil

¼ cup (60 ml) Kefir (See page 36.)

1½ tablespoons (25 ml) white balsamic vinegar

1½ teaspoons freshly squeezed lemon juice

¼ teaspoon Dijon mustard

½ of a red Bartlett pear, peeled, cored, and diced

¼ cup (30 g) crumbled Gorgonzola cheese

¼ teaspoon kosher salt

¼ teaspoon freshly ground black pepper

FOR THE SALAD:

1 head of butter lettuce

1 ripe avocado, pitted, peeled, and diced

½ of a large red Bartlett pear, quartered lengthwise, cored, and thinly sliced

⅓ cup (45 g) hazelnuts (preferably skinned), toasted and coarsely chopped

⅓ cup (40 g) sweetened dried cranberries

¼ cup (30 g) crumbled Gorgonzola cheese

The tender leaves of butter lettuce are topped with sweet pear dressing and savory crumbled Gorgonzola cheese in this recipe. Kefir is added to the dressing, enhancing it with enticing flavors. This combination of textures and flavors will encourage even the pickiest eaters to eat their vegetables.

- -

MAKE THE DRESSING: In a blender, combine the oil, Kefir, vinegar, lemon juice, mustard, pear, Gorgonzola, salt, and pepper and blend until smooth.

MAKE THE SALAD: Cut the lettuce into 4 wedges. Place the wedges on 4 salad plates. Arrange the avocado, pear, hazelnuts, cranberries, and Gorgonzola around the lettuce. Drizzle with the Gorgonzola Pear Dressing and serve.

NOTE: Although you can buy roasted hazelnuts, they're much more delicious when you roast them yourself. Preheat the oven to 350°F (180°C, or gas mark 4). Spread the hazelnuts in a single layer on a baking sheet. Roast the nuts for 5 minutes and then give the pan a good shake. Return to the oven and check the nuts again after 3 minutes. Shake the nuts again and repeat until the nuts are golden brown. If they have their skins on, transfer the nuts to a clean kitchen towel and rub vigorously to remove them.

Overnight Kefir Chia Coconut Oats

YIELD: 4 SERVINGS

- 2¼ cups (535 ml) Kefir (See page 36.)
- 1 cup (about 150 g) mixed fresh berries, plus more for serving (optional)
- ½ cup (40 g) oats (old-fashioned, rolled, instant, or steel cut)
- ¼ cup (21 g) shredded dried unsweetened coconut
- 2 tablespoons (26 g) chia seeds
- 2 tablespoons (40 g) raw honey
- 1 teaspoon vanilla extract
- Fresh mint, for garnish (optional)

This is a great make-ahead, take-along breakfast. It's hearty and filling with a surprising combination of flavors. Try this porridge with berries and fresh mint, make the seasonal variation of pumpkin in the fall, or the maple walnut or cinnamon apple anytime. Savor it in individual half-pint (235 ml) Mason jars for a perfect single serving.

Place the Kefir, berries, oats, coconut, chia seeds, honey, and vanilla in a 1-quart Mason jar and cover with a lid. Shake the jar vigorously and then refrigerate overnight. Serve in half-pint (235 ml) Mason jars. Enjoy garnished with additional fruit and fresh mint, if desired.

NOTE: There are many possible substitutions here. Use stevia in place of the honey, adjusting to your taste. Omit the oats and double the amount of chia seeds. Omit the coconut and increase the oats to 1/3 cup (27 g). Or use Yogurt (page 166) in place of the Kefir.

VARIATIONS
CINNAMON APPLE: Omit the berries. Add 1 cup (125 g) peeled chopped apple and 1 teaspoon ground cinnamon.
PUMPKIN PIE: Omit the berries. Add 1 cup (245 g) pumpkin puree and 1 teaspoon pumpkin pie spice.
MAPLE WALNUT: Omit the berries and honey. Add ¼ cup (30 g) chopped walnuts and 2 tablespoons (40 g) maple syrup.

 CHIA SEEDS

Chia seeds pack a lot of power in a tiny little seed. Indeed, the name *chia* means "strength" in the Mayan language. They are derived from the desert plant *Salvia hispanica*. Just 2 tablespoons (22 g) pack 10 g of fiber, 40 percent of the daily requirement, 6 g of protein, and 4,500 mg of alpha linolenic acid (ALA), an omega-3 fatty acid. Research shows that chia seed consumption is connected to improvements in heart health, including lower triglyceride levels, lower cholesterol levels, and lower blood pressure.

They work great when added to liquids because they soften and add a chewy, gel-like texture. Simply add the seeds and allow them to sit for at least 30 minutes. The seeds absorb about 10 times their weight in water!

Copycat Creamy Coleslaw

YIELD: 6 (1 CUP, OR 70 G)
SERVINGS

½ cup (115 g) Fermented
   Mayonnaise (See page
   156.)

¼ cup (60 ml) Kefir (See
   page 36.)

⅓ cup (115 g) raw honey
   or 67 g sugar

Juice of ½ of a lemon

2 tablespoons (28 ml) raw
   apple cider vinegar

1 teaspoon onion powder

1 teaspoon sea salt

¼ teaspoon ground
   black pepper

8 cups (560 g) shredded
   cabbage

¼ cup (28 g) Fermented
   Ginger Orange Carrots
   (See page 82.)

This delicious creamy coleslaw, a copycat recipe of your favorite fast-food slaw, is packed with a quadruple dose of fermented probiotics: Fermented Mayonnaise, Kefir, Fermented Ginger Orange Carrots, and raw apple cider vinegar.

Combine the mayonnaise, Kefir, honey, lemon juice, vinegar, onion powder, salt, and pepper in a bowl. Mix well.

In a large bowl, toss the shredded cabbage and Fermented Ginger Orange Carrots with the dressing. Cover and refrigerate for at least 30 minutes before serving to allow the flavors to combine.

✳ RAW APPLE CIDER VINEGAR

Apple cider vinegar that is organic, raw, unfiltered, and unpasteurized goes through two fermentation processes. This helps produce an incredibly healthful product, making apple cider vinegar a powerhouse of nutritional benefits. Here are some of these benefits:

» May fight heartburn. After a meal, simply mix 1 tablespoon (15 ml) vinegar into ¼ cup (60 ml) distilled or purified water and consume.
» May help improve digestion and bowel regularity, helping rid your body of toxins.
» May improve acne and other skin conditions.
» May improve stiffness and pain of joints.
» May help the body use fats as energy rather than store them as body fat.
» May help improve blood glucose levels and reduce side effects from diabetes.

Use only organic raw apple cider vinegar because this is the only type of vinegar that includes the healthful bacteria and nutrients. You'll notice that this variety includes sediment settled to the bottom. Be sure to use it unfiltered in recipes.

Buffalo Chicken Lettuce Wraps

YIELD: 4 SERVINGS

- -

FOR THE DRESSING:

½ cup (115 g) Fermented Mayonnaise (See page 156.)

¼ cup (60 ml) Kefir (See page 36.)

½ cup (60 g) crumbled blue or (75 g) feta cheese

½ teaspoon raw apple cider vinegar

¼ teaspoon garlic powder

¼ teaspoon onion powder

Sea salt and ground black pepper, to taste

FOR THE WRAPS:

4 tablespoons (55 g) butter, divided

2 boneless, skinless chicken breasts (about 8 ounces, or 225 g)

Pinch each of sea salt and ground black pepper

¼ cup (60 ml) Buffalo-style hot sauce

1 head of butter lettuce or small leaf lettuce, leaves separated

3 celery stalks, thinly sliced

¼ cup (28 g) Fermented Ginger Orange Carrots (See page 82.)

This meal contains all the flavor of your beloved Buffalo chicken wings, wrapped up in lettuce and drizzled with a probiotic-rich, creamy dressing.

- -

MAKE THE DRESSING: In a bowl, combine the Fermented Mayonnaise, Kefir, blue cheese, vinegar, garlic powder, onion powder, salt, and pepper. Mix well. Store the dressing in the refrigerator for up to 1 week.

MAKE THE WRAPS: In a skillet, heat 2 tablespoons (28 g) of the butter over medium-high heat. Lightly season the chicken breasts on either side with the salt and pepper. When the butter is hot (after 2 to 3 minutes), add the chicken. Cook until lightly browned and just done, 3 to 4 minutes on each side. Set aside to slightly cool.

When cool enough to handle, cut the chicken into bite-size cubes. Return to the skillet and cover with the hot sauce and remaining 2 tablespoons (28 g) butter. Over medium-low heat, bring to a low simmer and cook, stirring occasionally, for about 5 minutes.

Set a lettuce leaf on a plate, top with a bit of the chicken, celery, and carrots and then drizzle with the dressing. Roll it up like a tiny burrito and then repeat with remaining ingredients.

NOTE: As a fun alternative, serve the chicken, celery, Fermented Ginger Carrots, lettuce leaves, and dressing in separate bowls and assemble at the table.

Fish Tacos with Creamy Cilantro Sauce

FOR THE SAUCE:

¼ cup (60 ml) Kefir (See page 36.)

2 tablespoons (28 g) Fermented Mayonnaise (See page 156.)

2 tablespoons (28 ml) freshly squeezed lemon juice

2 tablespoons (2 g) fresh cilantro, chopped

½ teaspoon ground cumin

Sea salt and ground black pepper, to taste

FOR THE TACOS:

1 pound (455 g) flaky white fish, such as mahi mahi, about 1 inch (2.5 cm) thick (skin on or off)

¼ cup (56 g) coconut oil, melted

Juice of 1 lime

1 tablespoon (7 g) ground cumin

1 jalapeño, coarsely chopped

¼ cup (4 g) chopped fresh cilantro leaves

8 corn or flour tortillas

Shredded lettuce

Popularized in California, fish tacos are now available in many places. This recipe includes simple ingredients that are easy to find for a flavorful, zesty meal anytime.

MAKE THE SAUCE: In a medium bowl, combine the Kefir, Fermented Mayonnaise, lemon juice, cilantro, cumin, salt, and pepper. Mix well. Store in the refrigerator for up to 1 week.

MAKE THE TACOS: Preheat a grill to medium-high. Place the fish in a medium dish. In a separate bowl, whisk together the oil, lime juice, cumin, jalapeño, and cilantro. Pour over the fish and let marinate for 15 to 20 minutes.

Lightly oil the grill grates, remove the fish from the marinade, and place onto the hot grill, flesh side down. Grill the fish for 4 minutes on the first side. Gently flip and cook for an additional 30 seconds to 1 minute or until the fish is nearly opaque and flakes apart easily. Let rest for 5 minutes and then flake the fish with a fork.

Place the tortillas on the grill and grill for 20 seconds. Divide the fish among the tortillas and garnish with shredded lettuce and the sauce. Serve immediately.

Orange Pops

YIELD: 6 TO 8 POPS

- -

1 cup (235 ml) freshly
    squeezed orange juice

½ cup (120 ml) heavy
    cream

½ cup (120 ml) Kefir (See
    page 36.)

3 tablespoons (60 g)
    raw honey

½ teaspoon vanilla
    extract

The flavor of a creamy, orange pop is a classic summer memory. Recreate the experience with this recipe that uses the perfect amount of orange flavor from freshly squeezed orange juice. This may be even better than the original frozen treat. Who says you can't improve on a fond food memory?

- -

In a medium bowl, whisk together the orange juice, cream, Kefir, honey, and vanilla extract.

Pour the mixture into ice pop molds. Freeze for 4 to 6 hours, until frozen solid.

When you're ready to serve, run some warm water along the pop molds to loosen the pops and serve immediately.

NOTE: For the ice pop molds that I recommend, see the resources on page 185.

Chocolate Probiotic Ice Cream

YIELD: 6 (½- CUP, OR 70 G) SERVINGS

- -

2 cups (475 ml) heavy cream

1 cup (235 ml) whole milk

⅔ cup (67 g) sugar

½ cup (43 g) unsweetened cocoa powder

Pinch of sea salt

4 egg yolks

1 tablespoon (7 g) powdered gelatin

2 tablespoons (28 ml) vanilla extract

1 cup (235 ml) Kefir (See page 36.)

Frozen sweets, such as this luscious chocolate ice cream, hide the tart flavor of the kefir but retain all of the health benefits of the probiotics, creating a nutritious treat.

- -

In a large saucepan over low heat, combine the cream, milk, sugar, cocoa powder, and salt and warm gently.

Meanwhile, in a medium bowl, beat the egg yolks with a whisk.

When the milk mixture is warm to the touch, add the gelatin, stirring until dissolved. Remove the saucepan from the heat.

Slowly and gradually, pour about half of the warm milk into the yolks, whisking constantly. Then add the entire egg mixture to the remaining warm milk in the saucepan and return the saucepan to low heat, continuously whisking.

Continue to stir the custard base until it thickens, about 5 minutes more. Remove from the heat and add the vanilla extract. Refrigerate the mixture for 6 hours or until completely chilled.

Combine the chilled mixture and Kefir using a blender or electric mixer until smooth.

Churn the mixture in an ice cream machine according to the manufacturer's directions. Transfer to a container, cover with a lid or plastic wrap, and store in the freezer until ready to serve or for up to 1 month.

Pineapple Kefir Sorbet

YIELD: 4 (1 CUP, OR 75 G)
SERVINGS

- -

*1 whole pineapple, peeled,
    cored, cubed, and
    frozen overnight*
*1 cup (235 ml) Kefir
    (See page 36.)*

This sorbet is low in calories and uses nutritious, freshly cut pineapple and probiotic-rich kefir. With two simple ingredients and a quick run through the blender, enjoy this refreshing treat on the hottest summer day, or even on a blustery cold one.

- -

Place the frozen pineapple and Kefir in a food processor or high-powered blender. Blend until the consistency becomes creamy. You may have to stop several times and scrape down the sides of the bowl. Serve immediately.

NOTE: Put the mixture in a plastic bag with a corner cut off and squeeze out for a soft-serve ice cream look. Also, storage isn't recommended for this sorbet, so enjoy it right away!

Chapter 4

Dried Fruit *Chutney*

Spices, herbs, vegetables, and fruit are often put together in creative combinations to make chutney, a type of condiment often associated with Asian cuisine. Chutneys can be sweet or hot.

Dating as far back as 500 B.C.E., this pickled type of relish has always been simple to prepare. First created in India, chutney was initially a way of preserving foods. The recipe was eventually made popular with the Roman and British empires and then adopted by the American and Australian colonies.

Chutneys are served with many meals in India. Although the earliest varieties were prepared at home, commercially prepared chutney is readily available today. Some commercially prepared chutney includes added sugar, so check the label before purchasing.

The British took home chutney from India during the colonial era, and they favored the mango variety. They called it "Major Grey's Chutney," and it was widely available commercially, becoming quite popular. It was sometimes called "mangoed" vegetables or fruit.

Chutney was developed to keep fruits and vegetables shelf-stable, but its popularity declined with the advent of refrigeration. Refrigeration opened up a world of possibilities for storing perishable foods and fermentation was used less often.

Chutneys are popular again today. In the Caribbean and the United States, cooked papaya and mango chutney are popular. They are often paired with fish, ham, and pork.

Dried Fruit Chutney

YIELD: 3 CUPS (750 G)

- -

EQUIPMENT YOU'LL NEED:

Mixing bowl

Mixing spoons

1 glass quart (950 ml) jar with lid

Cheesecloth or cotton fabric square

Rubber band or string

INGREDIENTS:

1 cup (130 g) chopped dried apricots

½ cup (75 g) raisins

½ cup (60 g) sweetened dried cranberries

½ cup (80 g) chopped onion

¼ cup (45 g) chopped dates

2 teaspoons mustard seeds

2 teaspoons raw honey

⅛ teaspoon garam masala

1½ teaspoons sea salt

⅛ teaspoon ground white pepper

½ cup (120 ml) Whey (See page 168.)

¼ cup (60 ml) raw apple cider vinegar

¼ cup (60 ml) water

Zest and juice of 1 orange

If you don't have Whey (page 168), you can also make chutney with the liquid from another fermented vegetable, such as Sauerkraut (page 116) or Fermented Ginger Orange Carrots (page 82).

- -

In a large bowl, combine all of the ingredients. Mix well.

Transfer the mixture to a 1-quart (950 ml) jar and press down using the back of a spoon to remove any air bubbles. Cover the jar with cheesecloth and secure with a rubber band or string.

Allow to ferment at room temperature, out of direct sunlight, for 8 hours or overnight.

Stir, cover with an airtight lid, and refrigerate for 24 hours before using. The chutney will keep for up to 1 month in the refrigerator.

Cashew Fruit Protein Balls

YIELD: 24 BALLS

----

1 cup (100 g) raw cashews

½ cup (125 g) Dried Fruit
Chutney (See page 52.)

2 tablespoons (16 g)
vanilla protein powder

1 to 2 tablespoons
(15 to 28 ml) water

2 to 4 tablespoons (10 to
20 g) shredded dried
unsweetened coconut

Perfect for a quick snack or even a breakfast on the go, these high-protein balls are chock-full of delicious, probiotic-rich chutney and raw cashews. Use any vanilla protein powder of your choice; I prefer hemp.

In a food processor, combine the cashews, Dried Fruit Chutney, and protein powder. Process for 3 minutes or until crumbly and well incorporated. Add 1 tablespoon (15 ml) of water to make the mixture sticky enough to roll into balls.

Process for 1 to 2 minutes more. If the mixture seems too crumbly, add an additional 1 tablespoon (15 ml) water and process again.

Once a sticky consistency is achieved, roll the batter into 24 balls, about 1 tablespoon (15 g) in size. Set aside on a parchment-lined baking sheet. Spread the coconut on a plate and roll each ball in the coconut to coat.

Place the balls in the refrigerator or freezer to set for 30 minutes. Store, covered, in the refrigerator or freezer.

Fruit, Nut, and Gorgonzola Quinoa Salad

YIELD: 4 SERVINGS

- -

FOR THE VINAIGRETTE:

¼ cup (60 ml) apple cider
   or apple juice

1 tablespoon (15 ml) raw
   apple cider vinegar

1 tablespoon (20 g) raw
   honey

1 teaspoon Dijon mustard

Sea salt and ground black
   pepper, to taste

2 tablespoons (28 ml)
   extra-virgin olive oil

FOR THE SALAD:

1 cup (185 g) cooked and
   cooled quinoa

½ cup (125 g) Dried Fruit
   Chutney (See page 52.)

⅓ cup (40 g) crumbled
   Gorgonzola cheese

¼ cup (28 g) chopped
   pecans

1 celery stalk, thinly
   sliced

You can save time on meal preparation (and money, too!) by doubling the recipe to have extra to serve all week long. Make the quinoa the night before and assemble the rest of the ingredients in just minutes the next day.

- -

MAKE THE VINAIGRETTE: In a small bowl, whisk together the apple cider, vinegar, honey, mustard, salt, and pepper. While whisking, slowly drizzle in the oil until fully incorporated.

   MAKE THE SALAD: In a large bowl, add the quinoa, Dried Fruit Chutney, cheese, pecans, and celery. Toss with the vinaigrette to combine. Serve immediately or refrigerate up to 1 day.

Crostini with Roasted Garlic and Chèvre

YIELD: 8 SERVINGS

- -

1 head of garlic

1 tablespoon (15 ml)
   olive oil

1 baguette, sliced into
   16 rounds, ½ inch
   (1.3 cm) thick

8 ounces (225 g) chèvre
   (goat cheese)

2 tablespoons (30 g)
   Crème Fraîche (see
   page 20) or Greek
   Yogurt (See page 168.)

1 cup (250 g) Dried Fruit
   Chutney (See page 52.)

These crostini make for an easy, yet elegant, appetizer to serve to guests. They also make a light meal for a casual night at home. Either way, they're delicious and rich in probiotics. Each of the components can be made ahead of time for quick assembly later.

- -

Preheat the oven to 425°F (220°C, or gas mark 7).

Slice off the top of the head of garlic. Place the head on a piece of aluminum foil and drizzle the olive oil inside the head until it is completely filled and just starting to run down the sides. Wrap tightly with the foil and place on a baking sheet. Bake until tender and fragrant, about 35 minutes. Remove from the oven and let cool.

Reduce the oven temperature to 375°F (190°C, or gas mark 5). Place the bread slices on the baking sheet and bake until golden, about 10 minutes. Remove and let cool slightly.

Meanwhile, in the bowl of a food processor, put the chèvre and Crème Fraîche. Squeeze the roasted garlic cloves into the bowl, discarding the papery skins, and then blend until creamy.

Right before serving, spread each toasted baguette slice with about 1 tablespoon (15 g) of the roasted garlic goat cheese and top with about 1 tablespoon (16 g) of the Dried Fruit Chutney.

Harvest Chicken Salad

YIELD: 4 SERVINGS

----

1 pound (455 g) chicken,
   cooked and chopped
   or shredded

1 cup (250 g) Dried Fruit
   Chutney (See page 52.)

½ cup (80 g) chopped
   red onion

½ cup (50 g) chopped
   celery

½ cup (115 g) Greek
   Yogurt (See page 168.)

¼ cup (23 g) sliced
   almonds

Juice of ½ of a lemon

½ teaspoon garlic powder

Sea salt and ground black
   pepper, to taste

8 cups (440 g) salad
   greens

This chicken salad is a perfect lunch or dinner option that can be made in just 10 minutes if you have cooked chicken on hand. Plus, it packs a double-probiotic punch with both fermented Dried Fruit Chutney and Greek Yogurt. Here, I serve it on greens, but it's just as delicious as a sandwich.

In a large bowl, combine the chicken, Dried Fruit Chutney, onion, celery, yogurt, almonds, lemon juice, and garlic powder. Season the mixture with salt and pepper.

   Arrange the salad greens on 4 plates. Divide the chicken salad among the greens and serve immediately.

Roasted Salmon with Spicy Apricot Glaze

YIELD: 4 SERVINGS

Coconut oil, for the pan

½ cup (160 g) apricot preserves

¼ cup (63 g) Dried Fruit Chutney (See page 52.)

1 tablespoon (15 ml) coconut aminos or tamari

½ teaspoon red pepper flakes

4 skin-on salmon fillets (about 1½ pounds, or 680 g)

Sweet, spicy, easy, and healthy, this will be your new favorite way to enjoy salmon. Serve with rice and buttered broccoli for a delicious and simple meal.

Preheat the oven to 400°F (200°C, or gas mark 6). Line a baking sheet with aluminum foil and lightly grease with coconut oil.

In a small bowl, whisk together the preserves, chutney, coconut aminos, and red pepper flakes until well combined.

Place the salmon, skin side down, on the baking sheet. Bake on the center rack until it is almost opaque throughout and the internal temperature reaches 140°F (60°C), about 12 minutes. Remove from the oven.

Turn on the broiler and move an oven rack 6 inches (15 cm) from the heat source. Lightly brush the liquid portion of the preserve mixture over the salmon. Broil on the highest rack for 1 to 2 minutes, until the glaze is bubbly. If desired, slip a spatula between the salmon skin and flesh to remove the skin and serve immediately with the chutney.

Tropical Endive Bites

YIELD: 16 ENDIVE BOATS

2 heads of endive

1 cup (250 g) Dried Fruit Chutney (See page 52.)

½ cup (75 g) crumbled feta cheese or chèvre

¼ cup (60 ml) olive oil

2 tablespoons (28 ml) red wine vinegar

¼ teaspoon ground black pepper

Hors d'oeuvre recipes can be complicated and time-consuming, but not this one. Here is a simple yet impressive-looking festive party food topped with dried fruit chutney, feta cheese, and a drizzle of vinaigrette. If you don't like feta cheese, creamy chèvre (goat cheese) would be a wonderful alternative.

Carefully cut off the bottom stems of the endive heads and peel apart the leaves.

Fill 16 large endive leaves with 1 tablespoon (16 g) of chutney and 1½ teaspoons of cheese. Arrange on a plate or serving platter.

In a shallow bowl, whisk together the oil, vinegar, and pepper or mix in a salad dressing cruet. Drizzle over the endive boats and serve.

Sautéed Swiss Chard with Fruit and Nuts

YIELD: 4 SERVINGS

----

1 bunch of Swiss chard

1½ tablespoons (25 ml) olive oil

2 cloves of garlic, minced

¼ cup (23 g) sliced almonds

1 tablespoon (15 ml) freshly squeezed lemon juice

Sea salt and ground black pepper, to taste

¼ cup (63 g) Dried Fruit Chutney (See page 52.)

This fun and festive dish is perfect for your holiday dinner. Savory Swiss chard pairs well with the tart (but not too tart) Dried Fruit Chutney.

Remove the stems from the chard and cut them crosswise into 1-inch (2.5 cm) pieces. Cut the leaves crosswise into 2-inch (5 cm) pieces. Keep the stems and leaves separate.

In a large skillet, heat the oil over medium heat. Add the garlic, almonds, and chard stems. Cook for 3 minutes, stirring frequently.

Add the lemon juice and chard leaves to the skillet. Cook for 2 to 3 minutes until the leaves are just wilted, stirring frequently. Season with salt and pepper.

Top with the Dried Fruit Chutney and serve.

Turkey, Brie, and Chutney Panini

YIELD: 4 SERVINGS

- -

½ cup (125 g) Dried Fruit
   Chutney (See page 52.)

2 tablespoons (30 g)
   Dijon mustard

1 tablespoon (14 g)
   Fermented Mayonnaise
   (See page 156.)

Butter, softened, for
   cooking

8 slices of sprouted-grain
   or gluten-free bread

8 thin slices of roasted
   turkey breast

4 ounces (115 g) Brie
   cheese, thinly sliced

1 cup (20 g) arugula

You'll be surprised at the delicious flavor combination in these panini. To ensure the living cultures of the chutney aren't destroyed on a hot pan, these panini have a step after cooking: Allow them to cool briefly and then open the sandwiches and spread with the Dried Fruit Chutney.

- -

In a medium bowl, combine the Dried Fruit Chutney, mustard, and Fermented Mayonnaise. Mix well and set aside.

Preheat a grill pan or panini press over medium heat. Spread butter one side of each bread slice. Make sandwiches by placing 4 slices of bread (butter side down) on the pan, then divide the turkey and Brie among the slices, and then top with the remaining bread slices, butter side up. Cook the sandwiches until the bread is golden brown and the cheese melts, about 3 minutes per side, pressing down occasionally with a large spatula.

Remove the sandwiches from the heat, gently open, and spread each with one-quarter of the chutney mixture and one-quarter of the arugula. Close the sandwiches, press together gently, and serve immediately.

NOTE: While the rind of Brie cheese is perfectly edible, it doesn't suit everyone's fancy. If you're new to using Brie, place it in the freezer for 30 minutes, and then easily trim away the rind and use the inner semisoft cheese as desired.

Sweet Mango Chutney Sundaes

YIELD: 4 SERVINGS

1 mango, peeled and
   coarsely chopped

¼ cup (50 g) sugar

¼ cup (60 ml) water

Juice of ½ of lime

½ cup (125 g) Dried Fruit
   Chutney (See page 52.)

1 pint (285 g) vanilla
   ice cream

Chopped pistachios, for
   garnish (optional)

You can find fresh mangoes year round! This tropical fruit is fragrant and has a unique flavor that makes this dessert extra special. Mangoes are healthful too; one fruit supplies nearly 50 percent of your daily value for vitamin C and nearly 25 percent of vitamin A.

In a food processor, pulse the chopped mango until finely chopped.

In a medium saucepan, bring the mango, sugar, and water to a boil, stirring until the sugar is dissolved. Reduce the heat and simmer, covered, stirring occasionally, until the mango is very soft and thickened, about 30 minutes.

Remove from the heat. Stir in the lime juice and strain through a fine-mesh strainer into a bowl, pressing gently on and then discarding the solids. Allow to cool to room temperature and then stir in the Dried Fruit Chutney. Refrigerate to chill thoroughly.

Spoon the chilled chutney over bowls of ice cream and serve as a sundae topped with the pistachios.

Chapter 5

Fermented *Ketchup*

Ketchup is the king of condiments. It's used on everything, including French fries, hamburgers, and scrambled eggs.

The invention of ketchup can be traced back to royalty in imperial China. It started out as a fermented fish sauce and didn't even include tomatoes. This sauce was used on long ship voyages because it kept well for extended periods of time. Over the years, a variety of ingredients have been used, some not so appetizing, such as meat by-products and fish entrails, as well as plain, ordinary items, such as soybeans. Eventually, the popularity of the sauce spread to the Philippines and Indonesia, where the British sought out and further popularized the salty, tasty sauce. Lore has it that the British adapted the sauce, creating the tomato-based recipe we are more familiar with today.

In the nineteenth century, ketchup evolved with even more adaptations on the recipe. Fruits such as lemons, plums, and peaches; vegetables such as celery and mushrooms; and even shellfish, such as mussels and oysters, were used. Typically, the recipes called for the ingredients to be boiled and then left out to ferment with added salt. The salt kept the bad bacteria from multiplying to dangerous levels. These recipe enhancements produced a highly flavorful salty sauce much like the ketchup we know today. It was then that a scientist declared that the very best variation of the sauces used "love apples," an affectionate term of the day for tomatoes.

Transforming a family-friendly, daily-use condiment into a fermented food is, perhaps, the easiest way to fit fermented foods into mealtimes. Even the pickiest of eaters won't know the difference.

Fermented Ketchup

EQUIPMENT YOU'LL NEED:

Mixing bowl

Mixing spoon

Whisk

1 glass quart (950 ml) jar with lid

Cheesecloth or cotton fabric square

Rubber band or string

INGREDIENTS:

2 cups (520 g) tomato paste

¼ cup (85 g) raw honey, (80 g) maple syrup, or (50 g) sugar

¼ cup plus 2 tablespoons (88 ml) Whey (See page 168.)

2 tablespoons (28 ml) raw apple cider vinegar

1 teaspoon sea salt

1 teaspoon ground allspice

½ teaspoon ground cloves

If you don't have fresh Whey on hand, you can use the brine from Sauerkraut (page 116), Fermented Ginger Orange Carrots (page 82), or Sweet and Spicy Tomato Mango Salsa (page 148) to make this recipe.

Mix the tomato paste and honey in a bowl. Whisk in ¼ cup (60 ml) of the Whey, vinegar, salt, allspice, and cloves. Continue blending until all the ingredients are evenly dispersed and the mixture is smooth.

Spoon the homemade ketchup into a glass jar, top with the remaining 2 tablespoons (28 ml) Whey, and cover with cheesecloth secured with a rubber band or string. Let sit undisturbed at room temperature, out of direct sunlight, for 3 days.

After 3 days, uncover the ketchup and stir it thoroughly. Cover with an airtight lid and transfer to the refrigerator for storage. You can use it immediately, or store it in the refrigerator for several months.

✳ HOW TO FERMENT STORE-BOUGHT CONDIMENTS

Fermenting store-bought condiments is a quick and easy way to sneak fermented foods into every meal. It's especially useful if there's a particular brand you prefer. All that is needed is 1 tablespoon (15 ml) of Whey (or vegetable brine) for each 1 cup (240 g) of ketchup, (176 g) mustard, or other condiment. For example, you'd add 3 tablespoons (45 ml) Whey to a 24-ounce (680 g) bottle of ketchup and follow the same process as for fermented homemade ketchup.

Horseradish, ketchup, mustard, and salsa can be left to ferment at room temperature for 2 to 3 days. Mayonnaise should be left for only 8 hours before refrigerating.

Hash Brown Egg Cups

----

1 pound (455 g) russet
    potatoes

Sea salt and ground
    black pepper to taste

Coconut oil or butter, for
    the pan

12 large eggs

½ cup (120 g) Fermented
    Ketchup (See page 68.)

Do yourself a favor: Make up a batch of these on the weekend for quick breakfasts during the week. They can be quickly heated up and served with fermented ketchup for a probiotic boost to start your day!

Preheat the oven to 400°F (200°C, or gas mark 6).

Bake the potatoes directly on the center oven rack until tender, 45 minutes to 1 hour. Allow to cool and then peel and grate them using the large holes of a box grater. Season them well with salt and pepper.

Grease a 12-cup muffin pan generously with coconut oil or butter. Scoop 3 to 4 tablespoons (45 to 60 g) grated potato into each muffin cup. Use your fingers to gently press the potato down the bottom and up the sides of each muffin cup to make a nest. Bake for 15 to 20 minutes until brown and slightly crispy. Watch to make sure they do not burn.

Allow the nests to cool in the pan and then crack an egg into each one. Sprinkle with salt and pepper and bake until the whites are set, about 15 minutes.

Serve the cups with a drizzle of Fermented Ketchup.

NOTE: If preferred, whisk the eggs before adding them to the nests, for a scrambled egg in the middle.

Thai Red Chili Chicken Wings

YIELD: 4 SERVINGS

----

12 to 16 whole chicken
   wings

1 cup (225 ml) Thai sweet
   chili sauce

¼ cup (60 g) Fermented
   Ketchup (See page 68.)

3 tablespoons (45 ml)
   rice vinegar

3 cloves of garlic

1 inch, (2.5 cm) piece of
   peeled fresh ginger

½ teaspoon salt

¼ cup (4 g) chopped fresh
   cilantro

Called *nam nam* in Thailand, Thai sweet chili sauce can be used with egg rolls, spring rolls, and many other dishes, but it's perfectly paired with these chicken wings. Hot from the oven, these chicken wings have a sticky, sweet, spicy glaze, with a probiotic punch from the addition of Fermented Ketchup (page 68).

Cut the wings into 3 pieces: drummette, middle portion, and tip. (Save the tips for making chicken stock. I keep them in a freezer bag in the freezer for future use.)

Place the sweet chili sauce, Fermented Ketchup, vinegar, garlic, ginger, and salt in a food processor. Pulse until smooth.

In a large bowl, toss the cut-up wings with half of the sauce to coat. Marinate in the refrigerator for 1 to 2 hours. Reserve the remaining sauce for serving.

Preheat the oven to 375°F (190°C, or gas mark 5). Line a baking sheet with aluminum foil and place a wire rack on top. Spray the wire rack with nonstick cooking spray.

Place the wings on the wire rack and bake for 30 minutes. Keep the leftover marinade for basting.

Remove the wings from the oven and brush the wings with the leftover marinade. Turn the wings over and brush the other side with the marinade. Discard any remaining marinade. Return the wings to the oven and bake for 30 minutes more.

Just before serving, drizzle the wings with the remaining reserved sauce and garnish with cilantro.

Sweet Potato Fries with Creamy Barbecue Dip

YIELD: 4 SERVINGS

FOR THE DIP:

¾ cup (180 g) Crème Fraîche (See page 20.) or sour cream

¼ cup (60 g) Fermented Ketchup (See page 68.)

1 teaspoon raw apple cider vinegar

1 teaspoon raw honey

FOR THE FRIES:

2 large sweet potatoes (about 2 pounds, or 910 g, total), peeled and cut into ½- by 2-inch (1.3 by 5 cm) sticks

2 tablespoons (28 g) coconut oil, melted

Sea salt and ground black pepper, to taste

This dish is positively addictive! Coconut oil adds just the right crispiness and flavor to the sweet potato fries. The Creamy Barbecue Dip is velvety and sweet, an ideal pairing for the crisp sweet potatoes. Adults and kids alike will dig in to this healthful recipe.

Preheat the oven to 450°F (230°C, or gas mark 8). Line 2 baking sheets with parchment paper.

MAKE THE CREAMY BARBECUE DIP: In a small bowl, combine the Crème Fraîche, Fermented Ketchup, vinegar, and honey and mix well. Store in the refrigerator until ready to serve.

MAKE THE FRIES: Divide the potatoes among the prepared baking sheets. Toss with the oil, and season with salt and pepper. Arrange in a single layer, without overlapping.

Roast, tossing once, until tender and starting to brown, 25 to 30 minutes.

Season with salt and pepper and serve warm with the dip.

Sweet and Spicy Taco Salad

YIELD: 4 SERVINGS

FOR THE DRESSING:

¼ cup (60 g) Fermented Ketchup (See page 68.)

½ cup (120 ml) avocado oil or olive oil

2 tablespoons (28 ml) raw apple cider vinegar

2 tablespoons (40 g) raw honey

2 tablespoons (20 g) finely chopped onion

1 small clove of garlic, pressed or minced

½ teaspoon sea salt

⅛ teaspoon ground black pepper

FOR THE SALAD:

1 pound (455 g) ground beef

1 medium-large head of iceberg lettuce, chopped into bite-size pieces

2 medium-large tomatoes, diced

1 cup (177 g) cooked kidney beans (drained and rinsed, if canned)

½ cup (70 g) black olives, sliced

1 cup (115 g) shredded Cheddar cheese

2 cups (126 g) lightly crumbled plantain chips or corn tortilla chips

My mom made taco salad for as long as I can remember. Her original recipe included nacho cheese–flavored corn chips and bottled dressing. By switching to packaged plantain chips and a homemade honey French dressing, one of our family's favorite salads is now healthy and even more delicious!

MAKE THE DRESSING: In a blender or food processor, combine all the dressing ingredients and blend until smooth. Store the dressing in the refrigerator until ready to use or for up to 1 week.

MAKE THE SALAD: In a large skillet over medium heat, brown the beef, breaking it up into pieces with a wooden spoon. Remove from the heat and let the beef cool slightly.

In a large serving bowl, combine the lettuce, tomatoes, beans, olives, cheese, and ground beef. When ready to serve, add the chips and dressing and toss to coat.

Tangy Spring Spinach Salad with Grilled Chicken

YIELD: 4 SERVINGS

FOR THE CHICKEN:

1 pound (455 g) boneless,
  skinless chicken breasts
  or thighs

Sea salt and ground
  black pepper, to taste

FOR THE DRESSING:

1 cup (235 ml) avocado oil
  or olive oil

½ cup (100 g) sugar

½ cup (120 ml) raw apple
  cider vinegar

⅓ cup (75 g) Fermented
  Ketchup (See page 68.)

2 tablespoons (28 ml)
  Worcestershire sauce

1 small onion, chopped

FOR THE SALAD:

1 pound (455 g) fresh
  spinach, torn into bite-
  size pieces

8 ounces (225 g) white
  mushrooms, sliced

8 slices of bacon, cooked
  and crumbled

4 hard-boiled eggs, peeled
  and quartered

1 can (4-ounce, or
  115 g) can of sliced
  water chestnuts,
  drained

Spinach salad is a delicious way to increase your green vegetable consumption. Topping it with grilled chicken makes it a quick and easy weeknight meal.

MAKE THE CHICKEN: Preheat a grill to medium. Lightly season the chicken with salt and pepper. Grill, turning occasionally, until cooked through, about 15 minutes. Set aside.

MAKE THE DRESSING: In a blender or food processor, combine the oil, sugar, vinegar, Fermented Ketchup, Worcestershire sauce, and onion and process until smooth.

MAKE THE SALAD: When ready to serve, slice the chicken. In a large bowl, toss together the spinach, mushrooms, bacon, eggs, and water chestnuts. Toss with the dressing. Top with the sliced chicken and serve.

Turkey Meat Loaf "Cupcakes"

YIELD: 12 SERVINGS

FOR THE "FROSTING":

1 pound (455 g) Yukon
    gold potatoes, peeled
    and cubed

2 large cloves of garlic,
    peeled and halved

¼ cup (60 g) Crème
    Fraîche (See page 20.)

2 tablespoons (28 g)
    butter

Sea salt and ground black
    pepper, to taste

FOR THE "CUPCAKES":

1½ pounds (680 g)
    ground turkey

1 cup (120 g) grated
    zucchini, all moisture
    squeezed out with a
    paper towel

½ cup (35 g) finely
    chopped white
    mushrooms

2 tablespoons (20 g)
    minced onion

1 egg

1 teaspoon sea salt

½ cup (120 g) Fermented
    Ketchup (See page 68.)

The dinner "party" starts right now with Turkey Meat Loaf "Cupcakes" with mashed potato frosting! Probiotic-rich mashed potatoes with a side of Fermented Ketchup makes for a savory and hearty meal.

MAKE THE "FROSTING": Put the potatoes and garlic in a large pot with a large pinch of salt and enough water to cover. Bring to a boil over high heat. Cover, reduce the heat to medium, and simmer for 20 minutes or until the potatoes are tender. Drain and return the potatoes and garlic to the pot. Add the Crème Fraîche and butter. Using a potato masher or hand blender, mash until smooth. Season with salt and pepper.

Meanwhile, preheat the oven to 350°F (180°C, or gas mark 4). Line a 12-cup muffin pan with foil liners.

MAKE THE "CUPCAKES": In a large bowl, mix the turkey, zucchini, mushrooms, onion, egg, and salt. Divide the meat loaf mixture among the muffin cups, filling them to the top and making sure they are flat on top.

Bake, uncovered, for 18 to 20 minutes until cooked through (160°F, or 70°C). Remove the individual meat loaves from the muffin cups and place on a serving dish.

Top each Meat Loaf "Cupcake" with a light layer of Fermented Ketchup and a dollop of mashed potato "frosting." Serve immediately.

Shrimp Cocktail

YIELD: 8 SERVINGS

- -

FOR THE COCKTAIL SAUCE:

1 cup (240 g) Fermented Ketchup (See page 68.)

¼ cup (60 g) prepared horseradish

Juice of ½ of a lemon

½ teaspoon Worcestershire sauce

FOR THE SHRIMP:

1 lemon, halved

1 onion, quartered

10 whole black peppercorns

1 bay leaf

2 tablespoons (30 g) sea salt

2 pounds (910 g) large, shell-on, wild-caught shrimp

This recipe for homemade cocktail sauce is so easy and delicious that you'll never want to buy jarred cocktail sauce again. Chances are, you have most of the ingredients in your refrigerator already. NOTE: You can poach the shrimp 1 day ahead. Cover and chill.

- -

MAKE THE COCKTAIL SAUCE: In a bowl, combine the Fermented Ketchup, horseradish, lemon juice, and Worcestershire sauce. Mix well. Refrigerate until ready to serve or for up to 1 week.

MAKE THE SHRIMP: Fill a large pot three-quarters full with water; squeeze the juice from the lemon halves into the pot and add the lemon halves. Add the onion, peppercorns, bay leaf, and salt to the pot. Bring to a boil over high heat and then reduce the heat to medium. Simmer for 5 minutes to allow the flavors to blend.

Meanwhile, fill a large bowl with ice water.

Add the shrimp to the pot and cook until just opaque in the center, about 2 to 3 minutes. Drain and transfer the shrimp to the bowl of ice water to stop the cooking; let cool. Drain again. Peel and devein the shrimp, leaving the tails intact.

Arrange the shrimp over a bed of ice and serve with the cocktail sauce.

Burger Stacks with Secret Sauce

YIELD: 4 SERVINGS

FOR THE SECRET SAUCE:

½ cup (123 g) Fermented Sweet Pickle Relish (See page 132.)

¼ cup (60 g) Greek Yogurt (see page 168) or Crème Fraîche (See page 20.)

¼ cup (63 g) Dried Fruit Chutney (See page 52.)

¼ cup (60 g) Fermented Ketchup (See page 68.)

FOR THE BURGER STACKS:

8 ground beef burger patties (4 ounces, or 115 g each)

Sea salt and ground black pepper, to taste

8 slices of Cheddar, Swiss, or provolone cheese

8 large lettuce leaves

1 medium tomato, sliced

1 medium onion, sliced

½ cup (78 g) sliced pickles

Take burgers to a whole new level. Serve them on a bed of cool and crispy lettuce, topped with the most delicious secret sauce. Be sure to make a double batch of the sauce, as you'll be dipping everything in it. And nobody will guess it's packed with four fermented foods!

Preheat a grill to medium.

MAKE THE SECRET SAUCE: In a bowl, combine the relish, yogurt, chutney, and ketchup, and mix well. Store in the refrigerator until ready to use, or for up to 1 week.

MAKE THE BURGER STACKS: Lightly season the burger patties with salt and pepper. Grill over medium heat, turning once, until cooked to your desired preference. Top each patty with cheese and cook for an additional 1 to 2 minutes, until the cheese is melted.

Line each plate with 2 large leaves of lettuce, place 2 stacked burger patties on top of the lettuce, and top with sliced tomato, onion, and pickles. Drizzle a generous serving of sauce over the top and serve immediately.

Fermented Bloody Mary

YIELD: 4 (1 CUP, OR 235 ML)
SERVINGS

----

4 cups (950 ml) tomato
   juice

¼ cup (60 g) Fermented
   Ketchup (See page 68.)

Juice of 2 large lemons

1 to 2 tablespoons (15 to
   28 g) Worcestershire
   sauce

1 heaping tablespoon
   (15 g) prepared
   horseradish

2 teaspoons coarsely
   ground black pepper

Sea salt

Hot sauce

½ to 1 cup (120 to 235 ml)
   vodka

Celery sticks, for serving

Lemon wedges, for serving

Start the guest list now. This refreshing yet spicy Bloody Mary
is an essential for your weekend brunch party. Serve it with a
generous garnish of poached shrimp (see Shrimp Cocktail on
page 77) to make it a hearty meal in a glass!

Place the tomato juice in a large container with a tight-fitting lid.
Add the Fermneted Ketchup, lemon juice, Worcestershire sauce,
horseradish, black pepper, salt to taste, and hot sauce to taste;
shake vigorously. Taste and adjust for seasoning. The mixture
should be quite spicy.

   For each serving, pour about 1 cup (235 ml) Bloody Mary mix and
1 to 2 ounces (28 to 60 ml) vodka over ice in a cocktail shaker. Shake
well and pour into a glass. Garnish each with a celery stick and a
lemon wedge.

Chapter 6

Fermented Ginger *Orange Carrots*

When you think of fermented vegetables, you might think of sauerkraut. The truth is, with a little instruction, you can ferment many different types of vegetables for unique flavor plus a powerful probiotic boost.

Vegetables can typically be fermented in one of two ways:

SELF-BRINING: Lactic acid fermentation is the method for self-brining fermentation. The recipes here for Fermented Ginger Orange Carrots (page 82) and Sauerkraut (page 116) begin with shredded or grated vegetables. Salt is added to the vegetables, and they are mashed, rubbed, pounded, or left as is to settle in with the salt. This allows the salt to pull the water and liquid from the vegetable. This liquid combines with the added salt forming the brine that then coats the vegetables. This forms an anaerobic (without oxygen) environment for the fermentation.

BRINED: Saltwater brine is used in this method of fermentation. When you see a jar with pickles immersed in the liquid, this is an example of brined vegetable fermentation. The ratio for creating the brine is 1 quart (950 ml) water mixed with 2 tablespoons (30 g) salt. Seasonings are sometimes added to the brine.

Some vegetables work best with the brined method and others work better with self-brining. You could use either method with most vegetables though.

Leafy greens such as kale or cabbage brine best when grated or shredded first because large pieces may turn slimy. Carrots and other hard vegetables can be cut into larger pieces or grated, it depends on how you plan to serve the vegetable. Carrots (for example, Fermented Ginger Orange Carrots) are grated, and this dish can be added to a drink or tossed in with a salad.

Fermented Ginger Orange Carrots

YIELD: ABOUT 3 CUPS
(330 G)

EQUIPMENT YOU'LL NEED:

Large mixing bowl

Mixing spoon

Pounder (optional; See the Resources, page 184).

1 glass quart (950 ml) jar with lid

Smaller jar to use as a weight

INGREDIENTS:

4 cups (440 g) shredded carrots

1 tablespoon (8 g) finely grated fresh ginger

1 tablespoon (6 g) grated orange zest

1 tablespoon (20 g) raw honey

1 tablespoon (15 g) sea salt

¼ cup (60 ml) Whey (See page 168.) or brine from a vegetable ferment

Fermented Ginger Orange Carrots are a great starter recipe for learning to ferment vegetables. Carrots are naturally sweet and this is an ideal flavor to offset the sour, tangy, slightly acidic taste that is a natural flavor of the fermentation process. This can help you adjust to eating fermented vegetables. To shred the carrots, use the large holes on a box grater or a food processor. A rasp or other fine hand grater works great for the ginger.

In a large bowl, mix together the carrots, ginger, orange zest, honey, salt, and Whey.

Mash or pound the ingredients together to release their natural juices.

Place the ingredients in a quart-size (950 ml) jar and push down to make sure the juices cover the carrots and ginger, using the smaller jar filled with water or brine as a weight if needed. Leave about 2 inches (5 cm) of room at the top of the jar. (This is important to avoid juicy runover!) Cover very tightly with the Mason jar lid and let ferment at room temperature, out of direct sunlight, for 3 days.

Transfer to the refrigerator and store for up to several months.

Fruity Oatmeal Salad

YIELD: 1 SERVING

¾ cup (60 g) old-
  fashioned oats

½ cup (55 g) Fermented
  Ginger Orange Carrots
  (See page 82.)

½ cup (80 g) finely
  chopped pineapple

1 tablespoon (8 g)
  sweetened dried
  cranberries

Juice of 1 orange

Pinch of ground cinnamon

Pinch of ground nutmeg

Not only does this Fruity Oatmeal Salad make a healthy break-fast, it's also a delicious snack for any time of the day! Top with sliced banana, if desired.

Place the oats, Fermented Ginger Orange Carrots, pineapple, cranberries, orange juice, cinnamon, and nutmeg in a pint (475 ml) canning jar. Cover the jar with the lid and shake vigorously until well mixed. Refrigerate for 8 hours or overnight before serving.

Creamy Carrot Soup

YIELD: 4 (1½ CUP, OR
355 ML) SERVINGS

----

4 tablespoons (55 g)
  butter

1 medium onion, chopped

6 carrots, peeled and
  chopped

1 celery stalk, chopped

2 medium potatoes,
  peeled and cubed

1 inch (2.5 cm) piece of
  fresh ginger, peeled and
  finely grated

5 cups (1.2 L) chicken
  broth or stock

½ cup (60 ml) half-and-
  half

Sea salt and ground black
  pepper, to taste

1 cup (110 g) Fermented
  Ginger Orange Carrots
  (See page 82.)

½ cup (115 g) Crème
  Fraîche (See page 20.)

Fresh flat-leaf parsley,
  chopped, for garnish

Impress your dinner guests with a simple starter soup that's colorful and delicious. This one has a velvety texture and a fine, delicate flavor that is appealing to adults and children alike.

In a heavy pot or Dutch oven over medium heat, melt the butter. Add the onion, carrots, and celery. Sauté until soft, about 10 minutes, stirring often.

Add the potatoes, ginger, and chicken broth. Cook until the vegetables are very tender, about 20 minutes. In batches, carefully puree the vegetables and stock in a blender and return to the pot. Stir in the half-and-half and season with salt and pepper. Reheat, but do not boil.

Divide the soup among 4 bowls, and top each with one-quarter of the Fermented Ginger Orange Carrots, one-quarter of the Crème Fraîche, and chopped parsley.

Cabbage Apple Carrot Slaw

YIELD: 4 (1 CUP, OR 225 G)
SERVINGS

FOR THE DRESSING:

2 tablespoons (28 ml) rice vinegar

2 tablespoons (28 ml) olive oil

1 tablespoon (15 ml) coconut aminos or tamari

1 tablespoon (20 g) raw honey

Juice of ½ of a lime

1 clove of garlic, minced or pressed

½ teaspoon grated fresh ginger

½ teaspoon toasted sesame oil

FOR THE SLAW:

½ of a small head of red cabbage, shredded

1 cup (110 g) Fermented Ginger Orange Carrots (See page 82.)

2 medium apples (Pink Lady, Gala, Empire, or Fuji), cored and shredded

½ cup (8 g) coarsely chopped fresh cilantro (or flat-leaf parsley)

1 teaspoon sesame seeds

Not only is this slaw delicious on its own as a side, it's also crazy good as a topping on my Slow Cooker Kalua Pork Tacos with Pineapple Salsa (page 161).

MAKE THE DRESSING: Combine the vinegar, olive oil, coconut aminos, honey, lime juice, garlic, ginger, and sesame oil. Mix well and set aside.

MAKE THE SLAW: In a large bowl, combine the cabbage, Fermented Ginger Orange Carrots, apples, and cilantro. Mix well. Drizzle with the dressing and toss to combine. Refrigerate for at least 1 hour for the flavors to meld. Sprinkle sesame seeds on top just before serving.

NOTE: For a spicy slaw, add 1 thinly sliced jalapeño.

Thai Chicken Salad with Peanut Dressing

YIELD: 4 SERVINGS

FOR THE SALAD:

6 cups (420 g) shredded cabbage

1½ cups (210 g) shredded cooked chicken breast

½ cup (55 g) Fermented Ginger Orange Carrots (See page 82.)

¼ cup (36 g) chopped peanuts

2 scallions, thinly sliced

2 tablespoons (2 g) chopped fresh cilantro leaves

1 ripe avocado, pitted, peeled, and diced

FOR THE PEANUT DRESSING:

¼ cup (65 g) peanut butter

2 tablespoons (28 ml) coconut aminos

2 tablespoons (28 ml) rice vinegar

Juice of 1 lime

1 tablespoon (20 g) raw honey

2 tablespoons (28 ml) water

Put some spark in the traditional three-bean salad with edamame! The tender edamame add more fiber and protein than the typical green beans. Here, I've made it healthier with the addition of probiotics..

MAKE THE SALAD: Place the cabbage in a large bowl. Top with the chicken, carrots, peanuts, scallions, cilantro, and avocado.

MAKE THE DRESSING: In a small bowl, whisk together the peanut butter, coconut aminos, vinegar, lime juice, honey, and water. Pour the dressing on top of the salad and gently toss to combine.

VARIATION:

Use sliced almonds in place of the peanuts and almond butter in place of the peanut butter if you'd prefer to avoid peanuts.

Triple Bean Salad

YIELD: 8 SERVINGS

- 1 can (15 ounces, or 425 g) cannellini beans, drained and rinsed
- 1 can (15 ounces, or 425 g) garbanzo beans (chickpeas), drained and rinsed
- 1 cup (118 g) frozen edamame, thawed
- ½ cup (55 g) Fermented Ginger Orange Carrots (See page 82.)
- 1 or 2 jalapeños, seeded and chopped
- ¼ cup (4 g) chopped fresh cilantro
- ¼ cup (60 ml) raw apple cider vinegar
- ¼ cup (60 ml) olive oil
- 2 tablespoons (40 g) raw honey
- ½ teaspoon sea salt
- ¼ teaspoon ground black pepper

Three-bean salad is one of those quintessential American summer picnic foods. It's comforting, protein-rich, and easy to put together quickly with pantry ingredients. Here, I've made it healthier with a probiotic punch.

In a large bowl, combine the cannellini beans, garbanzo beans, edamame, carrots, jalapeño, cilantro, vinegar, oil, honey, salt, and pepper. Mix well. Refrigerate, covered, for a minimum of 3 hours, or preferably overnight for the flavors to blend.

Halibut with Strawberry Basil Salsa

YIELD: 4 SERVINGS

FOR THE STRAWBERRY BASIL SALSA:

1½ cups (255 g) chopped fresh strawberries

¼ cup (28 g) Fermented Ginger Orange Carrots (See page 82.)

1 tablespoon (10 g) finely chopped red onion

1 tablespoon (3 g) shredded fresh basil

Juice of 1 lime, plus more as needed

Sea salt and ground black pepper, to taste

FOR THE FISH:

4 skin-on or skinless halibut fillets (6 ounces, or 170 g, each)

Sea salt and ground black pepper, to taste

2 tablespoons (28 g) coconut oil

This refreshing, tangy salsa is a great accompaniment to halibut, red snapper, or salmon. The bright colors in the salsa really liven up this dish of fish. Round out the meal by serving it on top of a bed of baby greens.

MAKE THE STRAWBERRY BASIL SALSA: In a bowl, combine the strawberries, Fermented Ginger Orange Carrots, onion, basil, lime juice, salt, and pepper. Cover and refrigerate for at least 30 minutes or up to 2 hours. Taste and add more lime juice, if desired.

Preheat the oven to 425°F (220°C, or gas mark 7). Line a rimmed baking sheet with parchment paper or greased aluminum foil.

MAKE THE FISH: Rinse the halibut and pat dry with paper towels. (If the fish has been frozen and thawed, it will be quite wet, so be sure to dry it well.)

Season the fillets with salt and pepper. In a large nonstick skillet, heat the oil over medium-high heat. Cook the halibut, skin or skinned side up, for about 2 minutes or until the bottom is nicely browned. Transfer to the prepared baking sheet, browned side up, and bake for 5 to 6 minutes or until the fish is barely opaque and is just starting to flake when tested with a fork. Do not overcook.

Serve the halibut topped with the Strawberry Basil Salsa.

Chopped Sesame Chicken Noodle Bowl

YIELD: 4 SERVINGS

- -

FOR THE SESAME PEANUT SAUCE:

¼ cup (65 g) peanut butter or almond butter

3 to 4 tablespoons (45 to 60 ml) water

3 tablespoons (45 ml) sesame oil

2 tablespoons (28 ml) rice vinegar

1 tablespoon (8 g) grated fresh ginger

2 cloves of garlic

½ teaspoon sea salt

2 to 3 tablespoons (16 to 24 g) sesame seeds

½ teaspoon red pepper flakes

FOR THE NOODLES BOWLS:

4 ounces (115 g) soba noodles

Coconut oil, for cooking

1 pound (455 g) boneless, skinless chicken breasts, cut in half if large

Sea salt and ground black pepper, to taste

1 cucumber, finely chopped

Handful of fresh cilantro, finely chopped

⅓ cup (37 g) Fermented Ginger Orange Carrots (See page 82.)

Nutty sauce saturates hearty noodles in this one-bowl meal. The fermented goodness of the Ginger Orange Carrots (see page 82) adorns the crunchy cucumber for a rich texture experience. The ingredients are easy to find, and the assembly of this dish is simple, too.

- -

MAKE THE SESAME PEANUT SAUCE: In a food processor, combine the peanut butter, water, sesame oil, vinegar, ginger, garlic, and salt. Pulse until mostly smooth and then stir in the sesame seeds and red pepper flakes.

MAKE THE NOODLE BOWLS: Next, bring a pot of water to a boil and cook the soba noodles according to the package directions. Drain and set aside in a large bowl.

Heat a large skillet with a little oil over medium heat. Add the chicken and sprinkle with salt and pepper. Sauté until barely golden brown on the outside. Add about one-third of the Sesame Peanut Sauce to the chicken with a little water to thin it out. It might splatter, so turn down the heat at this point and have a lid ready. Let the chicken finish cooking in the sauce for a few minutes. Remove the chicken from the pan, let cool slightly, and shred.

Add the remaining Sesame Peanut Sauce, cucumber, cilantro, Fermented Ginger Orange Carrots, and shredded chicken to the noodles and toss to combine. Serve warm or cold.

VARIATION:
Use almond butter in place of the peanut butter if you'd prefer to avoid peanuts.

Raw Carrot Cake Bars with Maple Frosting

YIELD: 10 SERVINGS

FOR THE BARS:

1 cup (100 g) raw walnuts

½ cup (80 g) packed pitted dried dates, soaked in water overnight

⅓ cup (50 g) raisins

⅓ cup (28 g) shredded dried unsweetened coconut

⅓ cup (37 g) Fermented Ginger Orange Carrots (See page 82.)

½ teaspoon ground cinnamon

¼ teaspoon sea salt

FOR THE FROSTING:

¾ cup (105 g) raw cashews, soaked in water for at least 4 hours

2 tablespoons (40 g) maple syrup

1 tablespoon (14 g) coconut oil, melted

1 tablespoon (15 g) Crème Fraîche (See page 20.) or Greek Yogurt (See page 168.)

1 teaspoon vanilla extract

1 teaspoon freshly squeezed lemon juice

¼ teaspoon sea salt

Finely chopped walnuts, for garnish (optional)

These bars are vegan, gluten-free, and no-bake. Topped with a decadent cashew maple frosting, they're a perfect, healthy, probiotic-packed dessert or snack. Before you get started with this recipe, you'll need to soak your dried dates and cashews, separately, in water for several hours or overnight to make them soft. Drain the fruit and nuts and discard the water before using.

Line a small pan with parchment paper. (I typically use a 5 x 7-inch [13 x 18 cm] glass baking dish.)

MAKE THE BARS: Place the walnuts in a food processor and pulse until finely chopped (but not pasty). Add the dates, raisins, coconut, Fermented Ginger Orange Carrots, cinnamon, and salt. Pulse until the fruit is finely chopped and blended and the mixture begins to stick together, a couple of minutes, scraping down the sides with a spatula as necessary.

Spread the mixture evenly on the bottom of the parchment-lined pan and place in the freezer until set, about 1 hour.

MAKE THE FROSTING: In a high-speed blender or food processor, place the cashews, maple syrup, coconut oil, Crème Fraîche or greek yogurt, vanilla, lemon juice, and salt. Blend until very creamy.

Spread the frosting mixture evenly on top of the carrot cake, sprinkle with chopped walnuts (if using), and put back into the freezer for another hour.

When set, remove from the freezer, allow to thaw for a couple of minutes, and cut into 10 bars. Keep the bars in an airtight container in the refrigerator for up to 3 weeks or in the freezer for up to 3 months.

Apple Carrot Cooler

YIELD: 2 (2 CUP, OR 475 ML)
SERVINGS

- -

*4 cups (946 ml) apple
juice or apple cider*

*¼ cup (28 g) Fermented
Ginger Orange Carrots
(See page 82.)*

Juice of 1 orange

Ice cubes

Crisp, cool, and refreshing for any time of the day, this cooler is a
delicious and healthy drink for kids and adults alike!

- -

In a blender, combine the apple juice, Fermented Ginger Orange
Carrots, and orange juice and blend until smooth. Strain through a
fine-mesh strainer, if desired. Fill 2 glasses with ice cubes, and pour
the mixture over top. Serve immediately.

Chapter 7

Kombucha

Kombucha, a fermented tea with a pleasantly acidic and sometimes fizzy taste, has become popular in recent years among health enthusiasts. It first gained traction worldwide in the late 1990s, and it hails from teas originally served in Germany, Asia, and Russia. Some of the healthful effects associated with kombucha are longevity, immune support, and even weight loss.

A symbiotic culture of bacteria and yeasts, known as SCOBY, is the fermented goodness that rests atop a mug of kombucha. SCOBY is made with the tea leaves, sugar, and water, and the sugar feeds the SCOBY keeping the bacteria alive, multiplying and fermenting to make the culture. The unique flavor of SCOBY is described by some as pleasing yet vinegar-like or acidic. Sometimes the culture turns the tea a bit fizzy through the fermentation process. A small amount of alcohol is produced during the fermentation process and this alcohol along with lactic acid, acetic acid, and gluconic acid all fight the replication of bad bacteria in the culture.

Because the probiotic bacteria and yeast require the right environment to thrive, try making it at home to ensure the best possible result (providing you closely follow the guidelines for preparation). Fresh ingredients and proper storage are essential for the SCOBY to survive. Some studies show that commercially manufactured kombucha may lose some of its vitality due to improper storage and inconsistent manufacturing practices.

The SCOBY needs to stay clean and clear of mold, which can be a common side effect of poor preparation. Look for green, blue, or black coloring on your culture, which can signal mold growth. If you do spot mold, you will need to throw out the culture and sterilize your equipment before starting a new culture.

Kombucha

YIELD: 14 CUPS (3.3 L)

EQUIPMENT YOU'LL NEED:

Medium pot

1 glass gallon (3.8 L) jar

Cheesecloth or cotton fabric square

Rubber band or string

Instant-read thermometer

Reusable cotton tea bag, if you use loose tea

Straws

Long-handled wooden or metal mixing spoon

INGREDIENTS:

14 cups (3.3 L) water, divided

3 bags black, green, or oolong tea, or 3 tablespoons (approximately 8 g) caffeinated loose-leaf tea

1 cup (200 g) sugar

1 kombucha SCOBY

1 cup (235 ml) kombucha (This will come with your SCOBY.)

One of the nicest ways to start your kombucha tea is to ask a friend to share their SCOBY. Try to find a local co-op or try an online message board for folks in your area who share your interest in this invigorating tea. You may end up buying your own kit to start SCOBY but considering sharing yours with others. (See the Resources, page 184, for my recommendation.)

In a small pot, bring 4 cups (950 ml) of the water to a boil, remove from the heat, and steep the tea bags (or loose tea in a reusable cotton tea bag) for 5 to 6 minutes.

Remove the tea bag(s) and add the sugar, stirring to dissolve.

Add the remaining 10 cups (2.4 L) of water to the glass jar and then add the hot tea.

Your tea should be at approximately room temperature—no higher than 88°F (31°C) or you may kill your kombucha SCOBY. Use a thermometer to be sure of the temperature.

Gently add the kombucha SCOBY and kombucha and stir. Cover the jar with cheesecloth and secure with a rubber band or string.

Allow the kombucha to ferment undisturbed at room temperature (ideally 76°F, or 24°C) for 1 week.

After 7 days, you should see a new, cream-colored layer growing on the surface of your kombucha, which is a new baby SCOBY. While trying not to disturb it too much, dip a straw a few inches (about 7.5 cm) into your kombucha, cover the top of the straw with your finger, and pull out a sip to taste.

Taste your brewing kombucha once a day until your ideal kombucha flavor is reached. If it's still sweet, allow it to ferment longer. Most often my kombucha is done between 10 and 14 days, depending on the ambient room temperature.

When your kombucha is finished, with clean hands, remove your SCOBY, along with 1 cup (235 ml) of basic kombucha. Keep them together in a clean glass jar; this will be the starter for your next batch. It can be kept in the refrigerator, in an airtight jar or container, for several months until you are ready to brew again. After several batches, you will be able to separate the thickened baby SCOBY to share with a friend, along with 1 cup (235 ml) of basic kombucha so your friend can brew a batch too!

NOTES: Testing strips for pH can be used to verify that your kombucha is finished, which is when it's within the ideal range of 2.5 to 3.5. Although pH testing isn't strictly necessary, it can offer peace of mind to new brewers. See the Resources (on page 184).

When cleaning your kombucha jar and bottles, do not use antibacterial soaps, as any residue will prevent fermentation. Regular soap and hot water are sufficient.

Keep in mind that the sugar isn't for you; it's food for the bacteria. It needs sugar to grow and create beneficial probiotics, acids, vitamins, and antioxidants. With an average 10- to 14-day brewing time, the culture processes most of the sugar, leaving you with a healthy, delicious, and low-sugar beverage.

If you do not wish to do a second ferment (see page 100), simply place your finished kombucha in a sealed jug or jar in the refrigerator. Or, keep at room temperature and pour into a glass over ice when you are in the mood for a drink. It may not be as fizzy as bottled kombucha, but it will have all the same great nutrition and flavor.

 IS THIS NORMAL?

When handled properly, it's hard to ruin a kombucha culture. Here are some ways to tell whether your SCOBY is in good condition.

Healthy Culture
» Brown floating SCOBY that is a bit stringy and chunky
» Uneven SCOBY texture with bubbles, smooth and/or rough surface
» While brewing, SCOBY bobs and floats about in any direction

Unhealthy Culture
Use a new SCOBY if you detect green, blue, or black mold. Sterilize your equipment and get going on a brand new batch.

Kombucha Soda

YIELD: 3 CUPS (700 ML)

- -

¾ cup (170 g) chopped
  fresh fruit or all-
  natural, no-additive
  fruit juice (175 ml) of
  choice

3 cups (700 ml)
  Kombucha (See
  page 98.)

The second fermentation is what makes kombucha into a soda. After you have brewed your kombucha, seal up the brewed tea and allow the magic to happen. The fizziness is created during the time that the tea is sealed. The flavor combinations are endless, so feel free to experiment.

- -

To a glass bottle with a tight-fitting lid (see the Resources, page 184, for my recommendation), add the fruit or juice. Whatever the size of your bottle or however many bottles you're preparing, I recommend a 1:4 ratio of fruit or juice to kombucha (e.g., for every 1 cup [235 ml] kombucha, add ¼ cup [60 ml] fruit or juice).

Pour the kombucha into the bottle, leaving 1 inch (2.5 cm) of space at the top. Seal the bottle tightly and store in a warm, dark place, such as a kitchen cabinet, for 2 to 4 days.

After 2 to 4 days, move the bottle to the refrigerator. Once chilled, pop the top and enjoy your very own home-brewed kombucha soda!

NOTES: If you wish, you may strain out the fruit or small cultures that might have formed during the second ferment before drinking.

If you are reusing store-bought kombucha bottles or Mason jars, I recommend placing a piece of parchment paper beneath the lid to help make a tighter seal. Do note that it will likely not produce as fizzy a kombucha as bottling with swing tops, which make an airtight seal.

Carrot Chickpea Salad with Tahini Kombucha Dressing

YIELD: 4 SERVINGS

FOR THE TAHINI KOMBUCHA DRESSING:

*2 tablespoons (30 g)
  tahini*

*2 tablespoons (28 ml)
  Kombucha (See
  page 98.)*

*¼ cup (60 ml) extra-
  virgin olive oil*

*Sea salt and ground black
  pepper, to taste*

FOR THE SALAD:

*8 medium carrots, peeled
  and sliced on a spiral
  slicer or grated into
  long strips*

*½ cup (75 g) crumbled
  feta cheese*

*½ cup (8 g) fresh cilantro
  leaves*

*½ cup (120 g) canned
  cooked chickpeas*

*¼ cup (35 g) golden
  raisins*

This salad can be thrown together in just a few minutes. Kombucha adds some flavor to the tahini dressing. The fresh carrots provide crunch, the chickpeas add a creamy texture, and the raisins add a touch of sweetness.

MAKE THE TAHINI KOMBUCHA DRESSING: In a small bowl, whisk together the tahini and Kombucha. While whisking, slowly drizzle in the olive oil until all of the oil is incorporated. Season with salt and pepper.

MAKE THE SALAD: Divide the carrots among 4 salad plates or bowls. Top with the cheese, cilantro, chickpeas, and raisins. Serve drizzled with the Tahini Dressing.

NOTE: If you like, substitute sunflower seed butter for the tahini.

 RAISINS

Available in golden, green, or black, raisins are a surprisingly healthful addition to salads, cereals, baked goods, and snacks. Raisins are packed with flavor and healthful nutrients. Antioxidants can help protect your cells from damage and aging, and raisins are packed with these protective compounds. The fiber found in the fruit can help lower your risk for heart disease by lowering blood cholesterol levels. With a healthy dose of boron, a mineral strongly connected to bone health, raisins are an all-around superstar of nutrition. Plus they add just the right touch of sweetness to your day.

Lemon Rosemary White Bean Dip

YIELD: 2 CUPS (475 ML)

- -

1 can (15 ounces, or
   425 g) cannellini beans,
   drained and rinsed

2 tablespoons (28 ml)
   Kombucha (See page
   98.)

Juice of ½ of a lemon

1 tablespoon (15 ml)
   olive oil

1 small clove of garlic

½ teaspoon sea salt

¼ teaspoon ground
   black pepper

2 pinches of fresh
   rosemary needles, plus
   more for garnish

Snacks can be healthful! This standard white bean dip is improved with the added flavor of lemon and rosemary, and a probiotic addition from Kombucha. It is best served with crunchy fresh vegetables or even as a spread on a sandwich.

- -

Place the cannellini beans, Kombucha, lemon juice, olive oil, garlic, salt, pepper, and rosemary in a food processor. Pulse until creamy, about 2 to 3 minutes. Top with more fresh rosemary, if desired.

Beet, Grapefruit, and Chèvre Salad with Kombucha Balsamic Vinaigrette

YIELD: 4 SMALL SERVINGS

----

2 medium golden beets

2 medium red beets

FOR THE VINAIGRETTE:

1 tablespoon (15 ml) Kombucha (See page 98.)

1 tablespoon (15 ml) balsamic vinegar

1 teaspoon Dijon mustard

1 teaspoon raw honey

Pinch each of sea salt and ground black pepper

3 tablespoons (45 ml) extra-virgin olive oil

FOR THE SALAD:

4 cups (220 g) baby salad greens

2 grapefruits, peeled and segmented

4 ounces (115 g) chèvre (goat cheese), crumbled

⅓ cup (41 g) pistachios, chopped

2 tablespoons (8 g) chopped fresh dill

Think outside the box with this beet and grapefruit salad, which is hearty, earthy, and tangy, with a touch of light creaminess from the chèvre. You'll be sure to impress your friends at the next dinner party.

Preheat the oven to 425°F (220°C, or gas mark 7).

Place the golden beets and the red beets in separate foil pouches and set on a rimmed baking pan. Roast for 40 minutes or until tender. Remove from the oven and let stand until cool enough to handle. Peel the beets by rubbing them with your hands under running water. Cut the beets into ¼-inch (6 mm) slices.

MAKE THE KOMBUCHA BALSAMIC VINAIGRETTE: In a blender, combine the Kombucha, vinegar, mustard, honey, and a pinch of salt and pepper. While the blender is running on low, slowly drizzle in the oil until all the oil is incorporated. Set aside until ready to use.

MAKE THE SALAD: Divide the salad greens among 4 salad plates. Arrange the beets and grapefruit segments on top of the greens and then top with the chèvre, pistachios, and dill.

Drizzle with the Kombucha Balsamic Vinaigrette and serve immediately.

Chicken Satay with Cilantro and Almond Butter Sauce

YIELD: 4 SERVINGS

FOR THE SAUCE:

½ of a bunch fresh cilantro

1 inch (2.5 cm) piece of fresh ginger, peeled and coarsely chopped

1 clove of garlic

¼ cup (65 g) almond butter

2 tablespoons (28 ml) Kombucha (See page 98.)

2 tablespoons (28 ml) coconut aminos

Juice of 1 lime

1 teaspoon raw honey

Sea salt, to taste

FOR THE SKEWERS:

1 pound (455 g) boneless, skinless chicken breasts or thighs, cut into 1-inch (2.5 cm) cubes

2 tablespoons (28 g) butter or ghee, melted

Sea salt and ground black pepper, to taste

2 tablespoons (40 g) raw honey

Nothing says fun like food on a stick! This chicken is tender and honey baked. Serve with a side of your favorite grilled vegetables, (zucchini and eggplant pair nicely) and Fermented Ginger Orange Carrots (page 82). Your family will never guess it's so healthy!

Soak four 10-inch (25.5 cm) wooden skewers in water for 10 minutes (to prevent burning). Preheat the oven to 450°F (230°C, or gas mark 8).

MAKE THE SAUCE: In a food processor, combine the cilantro, ginger, garlic, almond butter, Kombucha, coconut aminos, lime juice, and honey, and process until smooth and creamy. Season with salt.

MAKE THE SKEWERS: Put the chicken pieces in a bowl or shallow dish. Pour one-third of the sauce over the chicken and toss to coat thoroughly. (Reserve the rest of the Cilantro and Almond Butter Sauce for serving.) Place the soaked skewers through the chicken pieces and arrange in baking dish.

Drizzle the chicken skewers with the melted butter and season lightly with salt and pepper.

Bake for 10 to 15 minutes until the chicken starts to brown and is cooked almost all the way through.

Remove from the oven and turn the skewers, coating them with any juices in the pan. Drizzle the honey over each skewer. Put back in the oven and bake for 8 to 10 minutes more until the chicken is cooked all the way through. Watch carefully so that it doesn't burn.

Serve immediately with the reserved Cilantro and Almond Butter Sauce.

Roasted Vegetables and Quinoa with Creamy Walnut Dressing

YIELD: 4 SMALL OR 2
LARGE SERVINGS

- -

**FOR THE ROASTED
VEGETABLES:**

½ cup (87 g) quinoa

6 small carrots, peeled
and halved lengthwise

2 portobello mushroom
caps, cut into ½ inch
(1.3 cm) thick strips

2 yellow bell peppers,
quartered and seeded

1 medium red onion,
sliced into ½-inch-
thick (1.2 cm) rings

1 tablespoon (14 g)
coconut oil, melted

Sea salt and ground black
pepper, to taste

**FOR THE CREAMY
WALNUT DRESSING:**

½ cup (50 g) walnuts

¼ cup (60 ml) extra-
virgin olive oil

2 tablespoons (28 ml)
Kombucha (See page
98.)

Juice of ½ of a lemon

1 tablespoon (20 g)
raw honey

1 teaspoon Dijon mustard

8 cups (440 g) spring mix
salad greens

¼ cup (30 g) sweetened
dried cranberries

Most of us would benefit from eating more vegetables, and the
easiest way to get more veggies into our diets is with salads. But
forget the boring salad routine. Roasted vegetables, quinoa, and
a creamy, nutty dressing take this salad to another level that'll
leave you satisfied and guilt-free.

- -

Preheat the oven to 400°F (200°C, or gas mark 6). Prepare the quinoa
on the stovetop according to the package directions.

MAKE THE ROASTED VEGETABLES: Divide the carrots, mushrooms,
bell peppers, and onion between 2 rimmed baking sheets. Lightly
drizzle with the coconut oil and sprinkle with salt and pepper. Roast
for 12 to 15 minutes until the vegetables are tender and lightly
browned.

MAKE THE CREAMY WALNUT DRESSING: In a food processor, process
the walnuts, oil, Kombucha, lemon juice, honey, and mustard until
smooth and creamy. Season with salt and pepper.

To serve, divide the salad greens among the plates. Divide the quinoa, roasted vegetables, and dried cranberries over the greens. Serve
drizzled with the Creamy Walnut Dressing.

Citrus Ginger Kale Smoothie

YIELD: 1 SERVING

- -

2 cups (134 g) fresh kale, stemmed

1 banana, frozen

1 navel orange, peeled and seeded

1 inch (2.5 cm) piece of fresh ginger, peeled

1 cup (235 ml) Kombucha Soda (See page 100.)

Orange slice, for garnish (optional)

Everyone is talking about green smoothies and maybe you've wanted to see what all the fuss is about. Here's your chance! Can something green and healthy taste that good? Don't take my word for it, try it, and you be the judge.

- -

Place the kale, banana, orange, and ginger in a blender and blend until smooth, stopping to scrape down the sides of the pitcher as needed.

Add the Kombucha and blend again until smooth. Serve with a slice of orange for garnish, if desired.

NOTE: Add plain or vanilla protein powder as desired. I suggest collagen peptides. (See the Resources, page 185.)

 GINGER

Thousands of years as a home remedy in Asian medicine can't be wrong. Ginger is healthful and versatile.

Long sought after for its ability to settle the stomach, studies support the efficacy of ginger to reduce feelings of nausea. Health professionals often recommend using natural ginger to help manage motion sickness, morning sickness during pregnancy, and nausea from chemotherapy. Studies show that ginger may be just as effective as medications often prescribed to treat nausea.

The anti-inflammatory properties of ginger may reduce the aches and pains of arthritis. One study looked at people with arthritis in the knee and ginger extract was found to alleviate knee pain while walking or standing. Or just try this spice for added fragrance and flavor.

Spiced Apple Cranberry Kombucha Sangria

YIELD: 3 QUARTS (2.8 L)

- -

2 oranges, sliced into thick rounds

6 whole cloves

1 bottle (750 ml) of white wine

3 apples, cut into thin wedges

2 cinnamon sticks

1 cup (100 g) fresh or frozen cranberries

1 cup (235 ml) apple cider

½ cup (120 ml) unsweetened cranberry juice

¼ cup (60 ml) brandy

¼ cup (85 g) raw honey

4 cups (950 ml) Kombucha Soda (See page 100.)

First used in Portugal and Spain, sangria is now a popular party drink everywhere. It adds festive flair to every celebration. In some cultures, sangria symbolizes passion and vitality, and with one sip of this recipe, you'll see why. Make this sangria the day before to let the flavors mesh.

- -

Stud the orange slices with the cloves by sticking the oranges with a toothpick to create a hole and then stuffing the point of a clove into it. Keep a few clove-studded orange slices aside for garnish. (Don't be tempted to use more cloves, or the flavor might overwhelm the sangria.)

Add the oranges, white wine, apples, cinnamon sticks, cranberries, apple cider, cranberry juice, brandy, and honey to a large pitcher or punch bowl. Give it all a good stir until the honey is dissolved. Allow it to sit for several hours or overnight in the refrigerator to let the flavors come together.

To serve, pour into glasses, taking some of the fruit for each glass. Top each glass with a generous splash of Kombucha soda and give it a stir. Garnish with a clove-studded orange slice.

NOTE: For a nonalcoholic version, omit the wine and brandy and use additional apple cider.

✳ HOW TO AVOID FAKE HONEY

Fake and impure honeys have become commonplace in the market today, despite many people's preference for 100 percent bee-produced honey. Unfortunately, unless you live in the European Union or Florida, you may not be able to trust "pure honey" labels. Because of the wide variety of honeys and large number of sugar syrups or other ingredients that manufacturers dilute honey with, it's imperative to be an educated consumer.

Whenever possible, buy local honey directly from beekeepers and ask them about the quality and purity of their honey. If you buy your honey from a store, check the label, but don't take for granted that you are purchasing pure honey. Look around the brand name or logo and at the ingredient list to check for additives or added flavors. Pure honey should have only one ingredient: honey.

Strawberry Lemonade Kombucha Ice Pops

YIELD: 10 POPS

- -

1½ cups (220 g) fresh
   strawberries, stemmed
   and chopped
1 cup (235 ml) freshly
   squeezed lemon juice
   (Use Meyer lemons, if
   you can get them.)
1 cup (235 ml) Kombucha
   (See page 98.)
½ cup (170 g) raw honey

Loaded with tons of fresh strawberries and a probiotic bunch from Kombucha, this kid-friendly ice pop recipe creates the perfect treat for a hot summer afternoon.

- -

In a blender, place the strawberries, lemon juice, Kombucha, and honey and blend well.

Pour the mixture into ice pop molds and freeze for 4 to 6 hours until frozen solid.

NOTE: If the pops don't easily release from the molds, dip them in warm water for a few seconds. For the ice pop molds that I recommend, see the Resources, page 185.

Chapter 8

Sauerkraut

Many of us automatically think of Germany when we think of sauerkraut, and that's probably because it's widely considered to be the national dish there. Instead, it's likely that it actually originated in China. The workers constructing the Great Wall of China were fueled by sauerkraut, and ancient Chinese leaders may have been the first to bring cabbage mixed with salt to Europe. The dish was quickly embraced by Europeans.

Europeans brought sauerkraut with them as they travelled by ship to the United States. They reportedly carried the fermented vegetable in a pickling crock. Sauerkraut supplied vitamin C fending off scurvy, which often plagued travelers on the long voyage.

The Amish and Mennonite communities living in the United States make traditional sauerkraut. Many of them are of Dutch or German descent, and you can still find the original recipe available in restaurants and for sale in markets in these communities.

Sauerkraut is made by finely shredding cabbage, mixing it with salt, and then allowing it to naturally ferment in the salted brine made from the juices the cabbage releases. Fully cured sauerkraut keeps for several months in an airtight container stored at 60°F (16°C) or below.

Raw sauerkraut is distinctly different from the store-bought, canned, or packaged varieties. Although many food manufacturers can or jar their kraut using heat to extend shelf life, raw sauerkraut is lacto-fermented and alive with good bacteria and probiotics.

Sauerkraut

YIELD: 1 TO 1½ QUARTS
(568 TO 852 G)

EQUIPMENT YOU'LL NEED:

Cutting board

Large knife, mandoline, or food processor with fine slicing disk

Mixing bowl

1 glass 2-quart (1.9 L) wide-mouth canning jar (or two 1-quart (950 ml) jars)

Canning funnel (optional)

Pounder (optional) (See the Resources on page 184.)

Smaller jar to use as a weight

Cheesecloth or cotton fabric square

Rubber band or string

INGREDIENTS:

1 medium head of green cabbage (about 3 pounds, or 1.4 kg)

1½ tablespoons (23 g) sea salt

Not only is sauerkraut delicious, it's also a bountiful source of nutrients. Rich in vitamins and probiotic bacteria, it's a surprisingly healthful dish. The fermentation process helps make the nutrients more readily available to the body. The cabbage is rich in fiber and, along with the good bacteria, it can help improve digestion. This recipe is low in calories and satisfying, too.

Discard the wilted, limp outer leaves of the cabbage. Cut the cabbage into quarters and trim out the core. Slice each quarter down its length, making 8 wedges. Slice each wedge crosswise into very thin ribbons using a knife, mandoline, or slicing disk in your food processor.

Transfer the cabbage to a large bowl and sprinkle the salt over the top. Work the salt into the cabbage by massaging and squeezing the cabbage with your hands. At first, it may not seem like enough salt, but gradually, the cabbage will become watery and limp—more like coleslaw than raw cabbage. This will take 5 to 10 minutes.

Take handfuls of the cabbage and pack them into the canning jar. If you have a canning funnel, this will make the job easier. Every so often, tamp down the cabbage in the jar with your fist or a pounder. Pour any liquid released by the cabbage while you were massaging it into the jar. If you like, place one of the larger outer leaves of the cabbage over the surface of the sliced cabbage. This will help keep the cabbage submerged in its liquid.

Once all the cabbage is packed into the jar, fill the smaller jelly jar with water and cover with a lid (to create weight). Slip it into the mouth of the larger jar. This will help keep the cabbage weighed down and eventually, submerged beneath its liquid.

Cover the mouth of the larger canning jar with a cloth and secure it with a rubber band or string. This allows air to flow in and out of the jar, but prevents dust or insects from getting into the jar.

Over the next 24 hours, press down on the cabbage every so often with the jelly jar. As the cabbage releases its liquid, it will become more limp and compact, and the liquid will rise over the top of the cabbage. If after 24 hours the liquid has not risen above the cabbage, dissolve 1 teaspoon salt in 1 cup (235 ml) water and add enough of this mixture to submerge the cabbage.

Ferment the cabbage for 3 to 10 days. As it's fermenting, keep the sauerkraut away from direct sunlight and at a cool room temperature—ideally, 70°F (21°C). Check it daily and press it down if the cabbage is floating above the liquid. Because this is a small batch of sauerkraut, it will ferment more quickly than larger batches.

Start tasting it after 3 days. When the sauerkraut tastes good to you, remove the weight, screw on the cap, and refrigerate. The sauerkraut can continue fermenting for 10 days or longer. There's no hard-and-fast rule for when is "done"—go by how it tastes.

While it's fermenting, you may see bubbles coming through the cabbage, foam on the top, or white scum. These are all signs of a healthy, happy fermentation process. The scum can be skimmed off the top either during fermentation or before refrigerating. If you see any mold, skim it off immediately and make sure your cabbage is fully submerged; don't eat the moldy parts close to the surface, but the rest of the sauerkraut is fine.

Store the sauerkraut in the refrigerator for several months. As long as it still tastes and smells good to eat, it will be. If you like, you can transfer the sauerkraut into smaller container for storage.

Mean Green Smoothie

YIELD: 2 (1½ CUP, OR
355 ML) SERVINGS

- -

2 cups (60 g) spinach

1 large cucumber, sliced

1 celery stalk, chopped

*1 green apple, cored
     and chopped*

*1 (½-inch, or 1.2 cm)
     piece of fresh ginger,
     peeled*

1 cup (118 g) ice cubes

*½ cup (115 g) plain
     Yogurt (See page 166.)*

*¼ cup (36 g) Sauerkraut
     (See page 116.)*

*1 tablespoon (13 g)
     chia seeds*

Juice of 1 lime

Juice of ½ of a lemon

This smoothie is the perfect blend of flavors—a tart green apple and herbal celery enhanced by the zing of ginger. You're sure to feel better after your first sip of this smoothie, especially because it's packed with fermented sauerkraut and probiotic-rich yogurt!

- -

In a blender, place the spinach, cucumber, celery, apple, ginger, ice, Yogurt, Sauerkraut, chia seeds, lime juice, and lemon juice. Puree for 1 minute or until smooth. Serve immediately.

Brussels Sprout and Sweet Potato Hash

YIELD: 4 SERVINGS

----

2 tablespoons (28 g)
   coconut oil

1 large sweet potato,
   peeled and cut into
   1-inch (2.5 cm) cubes

1 pound (455 g) Brussels
   sprouts, trimmed,
   halved, or quartered

1 cup (235 ml) water

4 large eggs

1 cup (142 g) Sauerkraut
   (See page 116.)

Red pepper flakes and
sea salt, to taste

Maybe your morning routine includes just a quick bowl of cereal. I promise you will appreciate spending a few extra minutes on this breakfast. The sweet potatoes caramelize right in the pan filling your home with a welcoming aroma. This dish will entice everyone in the house to get out of bed and make a beeline to the table for a delicious sit-down meal.

Heat the oil in a large cast-iron skillet over medium-high heat. Add the sweet potato and cook undisturbed for 4 minutes.

Stir the sweet potato and then add the Brussels sprouts. Cook for 5 to 7 minutes until the vegetables are deeply browned, stirring every 2 minutes.

Add the water and cook for 6 to 8 minutes until the potatoes are tender. Add additional water in ¼-cup (60 ml) increments, if necessary, until the potatoes are tender.

Meanwhile, in another skillet over medium heat, fry the eggs for 3 to 5 minutes until the whites are cooked through but the yolks are still soft. (See page 150 to learn how to cook eggs in a stainless-steel skillet.)

Divide the sweet potato mixture among 4 plates. Top each with Sauerkraut and an egg and sprinkle with red pepper flakes and salt.

Ahi Tuna Salad with Miso-Wasabi Dressing

YIELD: 2 SERVINGS

FOR THE MISO-WASABI DRESSING:

2 teaspoons rice vinegar

2 teaspoons white miso

½ teaspoon wasabi powder

2 tablespoons (28 ml) extra-virgin olive oil

FOR THE AHI TUNA SALAD:

4 cups (220 g) butter lettuce, torn

1 ripe avocado, pitted, peeled, and sliced

½ cup (55 g) Fermented Ginger Orange Carrots (See page 82.) or 1 carrot, shredded

½ cup (75 g) shelled edamame (thawed if frozen [59 g])

½ cup (71 g) Sauerkraut (See page 116.)

1 sashimi-grade ahi tuna steak (about 12 ounces, or 340 g), very thinly sliced

1 tablespoon (8 g) sesame seeds

If you like Asian flavors, you'll find a beautiful combination in this delicious salad, with even more taste and texture from the Fermented Ginger Orange Carrots and Sauerkraut mixed in.

MAKE THE MISO-WASABI DRESSING: In a small bowl, whisk together the vinegar, miso, and wasabi powder. While whisking, slowly drizzle in the oil until it's all incorporated.

MAKE THE AHI TUNA SALAD: Divide the lettuce among 4 bowls or plates. Top with the avocado, Fermented Ginger Orange Carrots, edamame, Sauerkraut, and tuna. Sprinkle with the sesame seeds and serve drizzled with the Miso-Wasabi Dressing.

Power Green Salad with Meyer Lemon Vinaigrette

YIELD: 4 SERVINGS

FOR THE MEYER LEMON VINAIGRETTE:

¼ cup (60 ml) olive oil

¼ cup (60 ml) raw apple cider vinegar

Zest of 1 Meyer lemon

3 tablespoons (45 ml) freshly squeezed Meyer lemon juice

1 tablespoon (20 g) raw honey

FOR THE SALAD:

4 cups (268 g) chopped kale

1 ripe avocado, pitted, peeled, and diced

½ cup (93 g) cooked and cooled quinoa

½ cup (87 g) pomegranate seeds

½ cup (55 g) chopped pecans

½ cup (71 g) Sauerkraut (See page 116.)

¼ cup (38 g) crumbled chèvre (goat cheese)

This kale salad is easy to whip up and is packed with powerhouse foods such as avocado, quinoa, and pomegranate seeds—and some fermented sauerkraut too! Combined with a wonderfully tart Meyer Lemon Vinaigrette, it's the perfect dish for a light but substantial lunch or dinner. Add your favorite kind of protein, such as grilled chicken breast or shrimp, if you like.

MAKE THE MEYER LEMON VINAIGRETTE: In a small bowl, whisk together the oil, vinegar, lemon zest and juice, and honey. Set aside.

MAKE THE SALAD: Place the kale in a large bowl. Top with the avocado, quinoa, pomegranate seeds, pecans, Sauerkraut, and chèvre. Pour the Meyer Lemon Vinaigrette on top of the salad and gently toss to combine. Serve immediately.

Classic Reuben Sandwich with Russian Dressing

FOR THE RUSSIAN DRESSING:

½ cup (115 g) Fermented Mayonnaise (See page 156.)

2 tablespoons (30 g) Fermented Ketchup (See page 68.)

2 teaspoons prepared horseradish

½ teaspoon Worcestershire sauce

Sea salt and ground black pepper, to taste

FOR THE REUBEN SANDWICHES:

2 cups (284 g) Sauerkraut (See page 116.)

2 tablespoons (28 g) butter, softened

8 slices of rye bread

8 slices of Swiss cheese

12 ounces (340 g) corned beef brisket, thinly sliced

Every good deli serves a classic Rueben sandwich. Now you can have the same sandwich at home. The Fermented Mayonnaise (page 156) used in the Russian dressing and the Sauerkraut (page 116) topping add probiotics to your sandwich. Toast the whole sandwich in the pan to melt the cheese and crisp the bread for a truly authentic deli experience. Serve with a side of Copycat Creamy Coleslaw (page 42).

MAKE THE RUSSIAN DRESSING: In a small bowl, mix the Fermented Mayonnaise, Fermented Ketchup, horseradish, Worcestershire sauce, salt, and pepper. Set aside.

MAKE THE REUBEN SANDWICHES: Using your hands, squeeze out excess moisture from the Sauerkraut and set aside in a bowl.

Butter one side of 4 slices of rye bread and place the slices, buttered side down, on a large piece of waxed paper. Top each with a slice of Swiss cheese and then divide half of the corned beef among them and add a second slice of Swiss cheese. Top with the remaining bread slices and butter the side facing out.

Preheat a griddle or frying pan on medium heat. Cook the sandwiches on one side until the bread is golden brown, about 2 to 3 minutes. Use a spatula to carefully flip the sandwiches over and finish cooking on the second side, about 2 to 3 minutes more.

Gently open the cooked sandwiches, and add ½ cup (71 g) of the squeezed Sauerkraut and about 2 tablespoons (28 g) of Russian Dressing to the inside of each sandwich. (We add the fermented foods after cooking so that the beneficial bacteria aren't killed during cooking.) Cut the sandwiches in half before serving.

VARIATION:
Ditch the bread and serve all the Reuben sandwich fixings on top of a bed of salad greens for a delicious Reuben salad!

Risotto with Prosciutto, Peas, and Wild Mushrooms

YIELD: 4 SERVINGS

----

4 cups (950 ml) chicken broth, divided

½ cup (120 ml) dry white wine

1 ounce (28 g) dried or 4 ounces (115 g) fresh wild mushrooms (See Variation on page 125.)

3 tablespoons (42 g) butter, divided

1 medium onion, chopped

2 cloves of garlic, pressed or minced

2 cups (400 g) Arborio rice or sushi rice

1 cup (150 g) fresh or frozen (130 g) peas

¼ cup (25 g) freshly grated Parmesan cheese

4 ounces (115 g) prosciutto, thinly sliced and chopped

½ cup (71 g) Sauerkraut (See page 116.), finely chopped

¼ cup (15 g) fresh flat-leaf parsley, chopped

When it comes to risotto, patience is required. Yes, stirring a pot of rice and broth for 20 minutes can seem tedious, but the finished product is truly worth it. The more you stir, the creamier your risotto will be, and the more complex and melded the flavors will become. Adding crisp sauerkraut at the end balances the creaminess with a big pop of flavor. This risotto will melt in your mouth.

In a medium saucepot, heat the broth, wine, and mushrooms over low heat. If the mushrooms are in large pieces or whole, chop them into smaller pieces, if desired. Keep the pot over low heat.

In a medium pot over medium heat, melt 2 tablespoons (28 g) of the butter. Add the onion and sauté until translucent, about 5 minutes. Add the garlic and sauté for an additional 2 to 3 minutes.

Add the rice and cook, stirring frequently, until it just begins to stick to the bottom of the pot, about 2 minutes. Add ½ cup (60 ml) of the hot broth mixture (avoiding the mushrooms until the very end) and cook, stirring the rice, until the liquid is absorbed. Repeat the process, adding the broth mixture and stirring until absorbed, until you've used up almost all of the broth mixture.

When you add the last of your broth mixture, with the mushrooms this time, also add the peas. Continue stirring until all the liquid is absorbed. Remove the pot from the heat, stir in the Parmesan, cover with a lid, and set aside. (You want to let it cool slightly so that when you add the sauerkraut, the enzymes are not destroyed.)

Heat the remaining 1 tablespoon (14 g) butter in a small sauté pan over medium heat. Add the prosciutto and sauté until it turns brown and crisp (like bacon), about 3 minutes. Remove from the pan and drain on a paper towel–lined plate.

Just before serving, stir half of the crispy prosciutto, Sauerkraut, and the parsley into the risotto. Garnish individual servings of risotto with the remaining prosciutto.

NOTE: For a dairy-free version, substitute olive oil in place of the butter and omit the Parmesan cheese. For a vegetarian version, omit the prosciutto.

VARIATION:

Any mushroom will work in this recipe, or they can be omitted completely. I prefer to use morel, chanterelle, shiitake, or black trumpet mushrooms, individually or in combination. They can also be left in large pieces so that you can flavor the dish but easily remove them for anyone who doesn't care for mushrooms.

✳ MUSHROOMS

When making a list of vegetables connected to anti-aging, mushrooms usually top the list. Used for thousands of years in traditional Eastern medicine, experts today still believe they have many health-promoting properties. They are thought to improve immune function, help fight incidence of cancer, and improve blood sugar levels in those with diabetes. Many people seek out red, purple, yellow, green, and orange-colored vegetables, which certainly are nutrient-rich and full of phytochemicals, but don't overlook mushrooms just because they're not brightly colored.

Wild mushrooms include morel, maitake, black trumpet, porcini, lobster, and chanterelle. Only forage for wild mushrooms with a mushroom-foraging expert until you are confident identifying edible mushrooms under the expert's guidance. Farmers' markets are great places to find fresh, seasonal wild mushrooms from avid and educated foragers. Most often, wild mushrooms are available dried in the produce section of many supermarkets or online. (See the resources, page 184.)

Sneaky Sauerkraut Sushi

YIELD: 2 SERVINGS

FOR THE RICE:

1 cup (200 g) sushi rice

1 tablespoon (15 ml) seasoned rice vinegar

1 teaspoon mirin

Pinch of sea salt

FOR THE SAUCE:

¾ cup (105 g) Sauerkraut (see page 116), drained

1 teaspoon tamari or coconut aminos, plus more for serving

½ teaspoon wasabi powder

FOR THE ROLLS:

1 large ripe avocado, pitted and peeled

1 medium cucumber, peeled and sliced into thin strips

2 scallions

1 carrot, peeled

8 (8 x 8-inch, or 20 x 20 cm) sheets of nori

Pickled ginger, for serving (optional)

Kraut has come a long way from its iconic hot dog topping. I've found that if you can add kraut to risotto, you can eventually add it to just about anything . . . even sushi.

MAKE THE RICE: Cook the rice according to the package directions. While the rice is still hot, drizzle the vinegar, mirin, and salt over it. Gently toss together. Let the rice cool completely before assembling the rolls.

MAKE THE SAUCE: Place the Sauerkraut, tamari, and wasabi powder in a blender or food processor and blend until smooth. Set aside.

MAKE THE ROLLS: Slice the avocado, cucumber, and scallions lengthwise. Use a vegetable peeler to cut the carrot into long ribbons.

Fill a small bowl with hot water. Lay a sheet of nori on a flexible surface, such as a bamboo sushi rolling mat or a tea towel lined with plastic wrap. Spread about 1 cup (186 g) of sushi rice evenly over the nori, leaving about a ½-inch (3 cm) border.

Spread ¼ cup (55 g) of the prepared sauce on the rice. Lay cucumber strips, a few carrot ribbons, half a scallion, and avocado slices evenly along the bottom edge of the rice. Moisten the exposed nori on the far edge with a little warm water from the bowl. Pull the mat up with your thumbs, hold, and tuck the fillings with all fingers. Roll forward and tuck the nori forward, while pulling back the mat slightly each time you roll forward. Just before you reach the end of the sheet of nori, moisten the end with a little more water. Continue rolling until you have a cylinder-shaped roll. Tightly wrap the bamboo mat around the roll and squeeze gently to seal the nori roll. Remove the mat and place the sushi roll on the cutting board.

Moisten a sharp knife with cold water and cut the roll in half. Cut each half in half, then each quarter in half, moistening the knife each time before cutting. You should now have 8 equal pieces of sushi.

Repeat the above steps until you have 2 rolls, or 16 pieces of sushi. Serve with pickled ginger and additional tamari, if desired.

NOTE: Mirin (a type of rice wine similar to sake, but sweeter) and nori (sheets of seaweed used to wrap sushi rolls) both can be found in the Asian section of most grocery stores.

Oktoberfest Quinoa and Bratwurst

YIELD: 4 SERVINGS

----

2 cups (475 ml) water

1 cup (173 g) quinoa
  (rinsed if your variety
  is not pre rinsed)

4 bratwursts

1 tablespoon (14 g) butter

6 cups (420 g) shredded
  Brussels sprouts

1 large onion, thinly sliced

⅓ cup (80 ml) raw apple
  cider vinegar

¼ cup (60 g) stone-
  ground mustard

2 teaspoons smoked
  paprika

Sea salt and ground black
  pepper, to taste

½ cup (71 g) Sauerkraut
  (See page 116.)

I've always had a healthy obsession with Brussels sprouts. If you are not a Brussels sprouts fanatic, or you simply feel like trying something else, plain cabbage would be perfect in this dish as well. Actually, one of my favorite cheats is packaged bags of coleslaw mix because they are usually just shredded cabbage and carrots. Buy shredded Brussels sprouts or put trimmed whole sprouts through the slicing blade of a food processor.

In a medium pot, bring the water and quinoa to a boil. Reduce the heat to low, and cover. Cook for about 15 minutes or until the water is absorbed and the quinoa looks fluffy. Drain if necessary and set aside.

In a large sauté pan over medium heat, cook the bratwursts until cooked through, 8 to 10 minutes. Remove the brats from the pan and set aside, covered.

Add the butter, Brussels sprouts, and onion to the pan you cooked the brats in. Cook over medium heat, stirring occasionally, so the parts touching the pan develop color, about 10 minutes.

In a small bowl, whisk together the vinegar and mustard. Add half of the vinegar mixture to the Brussels sprouts and cook for another 5 minutes.

Transfer the Brussels sprouts to a large bowl, along with the quinoa, the rest of the vinegar mixture, and the smoked paprika. Season with salt and pepper.

Divide the quinoa and Brussels sprouts mixture among 4 plates and top with 2 tablespoons (18 g) of the Sauerkraut and a bratwurst.

✱ QUINOA

Though it is considered a whole grain, quinoa is technically the seed of a plant related to spinach and beets. It is very high in protein, and the protein is the highest quality because it contains all the amino acids your body needs to produce muscles, tissues, and more. Quinoa is high in magnesium, which can help people with migraines and chronic headaches because it helps relax blood vessels. It is also a gluten-free grain.

Watermelon and Berry Cooler

YIELD: 2 (2 CUP, OR 475 ML)
SERVINGS

- -

4 cups (600 g) cubed
  seedless watermelon,
  chilled

2 cups (290 g) fresh
  strawberries, hulled

½ cup (71 g) Sauerkraut
  (See page 116.)

1 teaspoon fresh mint,
  chopped

Even the pickiest of eaters won't notice the kraut in this cool refreshing drink. It's completely masked behind the sweet combination of watermelon and strawberries. Surprise your kids with a special treat on a hot summer day by using this mixture to make frozen ice pops that are secretly full of fermented goodness. Or serve it up to your adult friends with a shot of vodka for a refreshing summer kraut-tail!

- -

In a blender, combine the watermelon, strawberries, Sauerkraut, and mint. Blend until smooth. Serve immediately.

VARIATION:
Feel free to experiment with other combinations of melon and berries—cantaloupe (640 g) and raspberry (250 g) are also delicious.

✳ **WATERMELON**

Watermelon is often viewed as a fun fruit to add to a picnic or summer celebration. But it's a nutrient-rich fruit with many health benefits, and it makes sense to include it often in your repertoire. It's rich in lycopene, a pigment that gives it its red color, which is a phytochemical linked to heart health.

» Watermelon is rich in vitamin A, which enhances immunity and is strongly connected to skin and eye health.

» It's full of vitamin C, which can protect you from viruses and infections and also fight the aging of your body's cells.

» Watermelon has vitamin B_6, which helps your body produce red blood cells, break down proteins that you eat, and maintain nerve functioning. Vitamin B_6 also helps produce antibodies linked to good immune function and fighting disease.

Chapter 9

Fermented Sweet *Pickle Relish*

First created in India as a delicious way to preserve vegetables through fermentation, relish is now popular nearly everywhere. Relish is typically made from chopped vegetables that are seasoned and fermented for several days. It can be sweet, savory, mild, or hot.

Relish is a broad category of food items that are served alongside a meal for the purpose of a condiment.

In the United States, the most common commercially available relishes are made from pickled cucumbers and are known as pickle relishes. Two variants of pickle relish are hamburger relish (pickle relish in a ketchup base or sauce) and hot dog relish (pickle relish in a mustard base or sauce).

In this chapter, we will be making a traditional fermented sweet pickle relish. Although it will taste similar to the jarred varieties you've been purchasing at the grocery store (most of which contain high-fructose corn syrup), this one is chock-full of nutritious real food and fermented for a probiotic punch. You'll get all the health benefits without anyone realizing you swapped in a fermented food.

Fermented Sweet Pickle Relish

YIELD: ABOUT 3 CUPS
(735 G)

EQUIPMENT YOU'LL NEED:

Mixing bowl

Mixing spoon

*1 glass quart (946 ml)
   jar with lid*

*Weight or smaller
   glass jar*

*Cheesecloth or cotton
   fabric square*

Rubber band or string

INGREDIENTS:

*3 cups (405 g) finely
   chopped cucumber*

*½ cup (75 g) finely
   chopped red bell pepper*

*½ cup (80 g) finely
   chopped onion*

1½ teaspoons sea salt

½ cup (170 g) raw honey

*½ cup (60 ml) raw apple
   cider vinegar*

*¼ cup (60 ml) Whey (See
   page 168.) or brine from
   a vegetable ferment*

*1 tablespoon (11 g)
   mustard seeds*

*½ teaspoon ground
   turmeric*

Sweet pickle relish is also a favorite, and it's so easy to make—just toss together the ingredients, cover, and allow the good bacteria to work their magic.

In a large bowl, mix together the cucumber, red bell pepper, onion, and salt. Place the mixture in a quart (950 ml) jar and press to remove any air bubbles.

In the same bowl, combine the honey, vinegar, Whey, mustard seeds, and turmeric and pour the liquid into the jar. Place a weight (such as a smaller glass jar) inside the jar to ensure the relish is fully submerged under the liquid.

Cover the top of the jar with cheesecloth and secure with a rubber band or string. Ferment at room temperature (roughly 70°F, or 21°C) for 3 days. Cover with an airtight lid and store in the refrigerator overnight for the flavors to combine. The relish will keep in the refrigerator for up to 1 month.

NOTE: If your ambient home temperature is colder than 68°F (20°C), create a warm fermentation station using the tips on page 17.

Avocado Egg Salad

YIELD: 4 SERVINGS

----

6 large hard-boiled
   eggs, diced

1 avocado, pitted, peeled,
   and diced

2 tablespoons (30 g) plain
   or Greek Yogurt (See
   page 168.)

2 tablespoons (28 g)
   Fermented Mayonnaise
   (See page 156.)

2 tablespoons (30 g)
   Fermented Sweet Pickle
   Relish (See page 132.)

2 tablespoons (13 g) finely
   chopped celery

1 tablespoon (10 g) finely
   chopped onion

Sea salt and ground black
   pepper, to taste

8 slices of sprouted-grain
   or gluten-free bread or
   4 cups (220 g) mixed
   greens

Full of protein, healthy fats, and fermented ingredients, this avocado egg salad is the perfect way to start your day. Whether served on toasted sprouted-grain bread or atop a bed of mixed greens, this breakfast will keep you full and focused straight through until lunch.

In a large bowl, combine the eggs, avocado, Yogurt, Fermented Mayonnaise, Fermented Sweet Pickle Relish, celery, and onion, and season with salt and black pepper.

Serve as a sandwich on bread or serve on a bed of mixed greens for a grain-free, gluten-free, low-carb option.

 WHY PASTURE-RAISED EGGS?

A 2009 study by *Mother Earth News* found that eggs from pasture-raised hens contain up to 126 percent of the recommended daily value of vitamin D. This is more than eggs from hens raised indoors and confined to cages. In fact, some estimates state that eggs from the pasture-raised hens contain up to six times more vitamin D.

There are many reasons to choose meat and eggs from free-range hens. These hens have a chance to go outside, roam around, soak up sunlight and produce vitamin D, and consume bugs and greens that help them produce very nutritious eggs. One way to find free-range hens and ensure that you are getting the most nutritious eggs is to visit a local farmer's market and speak to the farmer and ask questions.

Thai Chicken Lettuce Wraps

YIELD: 4 SERVINGS

FOR THE THAI CHICKEN:

2 tablespoons (28 g)
    butter

½ of a medium onion,
    chopped

2 tablespoons (32 g)
    tomato paste

2 cloves of garlic, minced
    or pressed

3 tablespoons (42 g) Thai
    sweet chili sauce

1 tablespoon (15 ml)
    Worcestershire sauce

1 pound (455 g) boneless,
    skinless chicken thighs
    or breast, cut into bite-
    size pieces

FOR THE SLAW TOPPING:

3 tablespoons (45 g)
    Fermented Sweet Pickle
    Relish (See page 132.)

Juice of 1 lemon

2 tablespoons (40 g)
    raw honey

2 cups (140 g) shredded
    cabbage

¼ cup (28 g) Fermented
    Ginger Orange Carrots
    (See page 82.)

Bibb or butter lettuce

Combining sweet and savory chicken with crispy slaw is the perfect, healthy, quick weeknight meal that's going to wow your whole family. Instead of serving the chicken mixture wrapped in the lettuce, you could serve the chicken mixture and slaw over rice or on a bed of salad greens.

MAKE THE THAI CHICKEN: In a large skillet over medium heat, melt the butter. Sauté the onion, tomato paste, and garlic until the onion is softened, about 4 minutes. Stir in the chili and Worcestershire sauces. Add the chicken. Cook, stirring occasionally, until the chicken is no longer pink in the center, 5 to 10 minutes.

MAKE THE SLAW TOPPING: In a large bowl, whisk together the Fermented Sweet Pickle Relish, lemon juice, and honey. Add the cabbage and Fermented Ginger Orange Carrots, mixing well to coat with the dressing.

Serve the chicken wrapped in lettuce leaves, topped generously with the slaw.

Ham Salad Spread

YIELD: 3 CUPS (680 G)

- -

1 pound (455 g) cooked
ham, chopped

½ cup (115 g) Fermented
Mayonnaise (See page
156.)

⅓ cup (82 g) Fermented
Sweet Pickle Relish (See
page 132.)

2 tablespoons (20 g)
finely chopped onion

2 tablespoons (15 g) finely
chopped celery

This is a great recipe to repurpose your leftover holiday ham in a brand new way. It's great as a dip, spread, or sandwich filling, and with my Fermented Sweet Pickle Relish, it's packed with probiotics!

- -

Pulse the chopped ham in a food processor until you have very small pieces. Take care not to overprocess.

Transfer the ham to a medium bowl and add the Fermented Sweet Pickle Relish, Fermented Mayonnaise, relish, onion, and celery, folding to combine. Serve chilled, as a sandwich spread or a topper for crackers or cucumber slices. It's also good served on a bed of fresh greens. The spread will keep in the refrigerator for up to 1 week.

NOTE: Add additional Fermented Mayonnaise if think your ham salad is dry. For a softer ham salad—more like the type you might purchase at a deli counter—use a meat grinder to grind your ham.

VARIATION:
Use turkey in place of the ham for a delicious turkey salad.

Sweet Pimento Cheese Dip

YIELD: 2 CUPS (455 G)

----

2 cups (240 g) grated
  sharp Cheddar cheese

¼ cup (60 g) Fermented
  Sweet Pickle Relish (See
  page 132.)

¼ cup (60 g) Greek
  Yogurt (See page 168.)

¼ cup (60 g) Fermented
  Mayonnaise (See page
  156.)

1 jar (4 ounces, or 115 g)
  pimentos, drained and
  chopped

1 medium jalapeño,
  seeded and chopped

½ teaspoon garlic powder

½ teaspoon onion powder

¼ teaspoon sea salt

½ teaspoon ground
  black pepper

This wonderful homemade pimento cheese spread can be used for grilled cheese sandwiches, as a spread for crackers, or served on top of celery sticks for a delightful snack.

In a medium bowl, combine the cheese, Fermented Sweet Pickle Relish, Yogurt, Fermented Mayonnaise, pimentos, jalapeño, garlic powder, onion powder, salt, and pepper. Mix well. Refrigerate overnight to allow the flavors to combine.

Serve with crackers or as a topping on celery sticks. Store any remaining Pimento Cheese Dip in the refrigerator for up to 1 week.

Salmon Salad–Stuffed Tomatoes

YIELD: 6 SERVINGS

- -

6 tomatoes (each the size of a baseball)

1 cup (215 g) flaked cooked wild-caught salmon

2 tablespoons (30 g) Fermented Sweet Pickle Relish (See page 132.)

2 tablespoons (13 g) chopped celery

2 tablespoons (20 g) chopped onion

2 tablespoons (30 g) Greek Yogurt (See page 168.)

2 tablespoons (28 g) Fermented Mayonnaise (See page 156.)

1 tablespoon (4 g) chopped fresh flat-leaf parsley

1 teaspoon horseradish mustard

Sea salt and ground black pepper, to taste

By using salmon in this recipe, you ramp up your omega-3 fatty acid intake up to nine times the amount supplied by tuna in a typical tuna salad recipe! You can make it with canned or grilled salmon.

- -

Remove the cores and carefully hollow out the insides of the tomatoes with a spoon, making space for a generous serving of Salmon Salad. Set aside.

In a medium bowl, combine the salmon, Fermented Sweet Pickle Relish, celery, onion, Yogurt, Fermented Mayonnaise, parsley, and mustard, and season with sea salt and pepper.

Fill each hollowed-out tomato with one-sixth of the Salmon Salad. Serve immediately.

Confetti Herbed Potato Salad

YIELD: 4 SERVINGS

- 2 pounds (910 g) Yukon gold or red-skinned potatoes (about 4 medium-large)
- 3 large hard-boiled eggs, peeled and chopped
- 2 celery stalks, finely chopped
- 1 red bell pepper, finely chopped
- 5 or 6 scallions (white and green parts), finely chopped
- ¼ cup (61 g) Fermented Sweet Pickle Relish (See page 132.)
- 2 tablespoons (8 g) chopped fresh flat-leaf parsley
- 2 tablespoons (6 g) chopped fresh chives
- 1 tablespoon (15 g) Dijon mustard
- 1 teaspoon prepared horseradish
- 1 cup (225 g) Fermented Mayonnaise (See page 156.), or more as needed
- Sea salt and ground black pepper, to taste

Picnic-ready dishes like macaroni and potato salad have been around forever. They can be made healthier with fresh ingredients and fermented mayonnaise that supply a good dose of probiotic bacteria. The flavors combine to make the perfect side dish for your next cookout, especially when filled with the flavors of freshly chopped herbs. Although most everyone enjoys their potato salad chilled, I prefer mine right after it's been mixed and the potatoes are still warm!

Bring a large pot of salted water to a boil and cook the potatoes for 10 to 15 minutes until the potatoes are easily pierced with a paring knife. Drain and let cool until just cool enough to handle. Peel the skins from the potatoes and cut into bite-size pieces.

In a large bowl, combine the cooked potatoes, eggs, celery, red bell pepper, scallions, Fermented Sweet Pickle Relish, parsley, chives, mustard, horseradish, and Fermented Mayonnaise, and stir to coat, using additional mayonnaise if needed. Season with sea salt and black pepper.

Serve right away while still warm, or refrigerate and serve chilled.

✳ HORSERADISH

Horseradish is rich in glucosinolates, which are thought to help detoxify carcinogens and may suppress tumor growth.

Horseradish root is rich in vitamin C, an antioxidant. It boosts immunity and can help fight against infections and viruses, including colds, the bacterial infection that causes bronchitis, and urinary tract infections. The glucosinolates and other derivatives of this compound found in horseradish root are also thought to protect against colon and rectal cancer, and reduce the risk of other cancers.

Horseradish root aids in the secretion of digestive enzymes from the intestine as well as salivary and gastric enzymes.

Swiss Mushroom Melt

YIELD: 4 SANDWICHES

FOR THE SANDWICH SPREAD:

3 tablespoons (45 g) Fermented Sweet Pickle Relish (See page 132.)

3 tablespoons (42 g) Fermented Mayonnaise (See page 156.)

1 tablespoon (15 g) Fermented Ketchup (See page 68.)

FOR THE SWISS MUSHROOM MELT:

⅓ cup (75 g) butter, divided

8 ounces (225 g) white mushrooms, sliced

1 teaspoon Worcestershire sauce

½ teaspoon garlic powder

¼ teaspoon dried thyme

Sea salt and ground black pepper, to taste

8 slices of sprouted-grain or gluten-free bread

8 slices of Swiss cheese

4 slices of provolone cheese

Flavorful mushrooms surrounded by gooey melted Swiss cheese: Can you go wrong? To make it a heartier meal, add a hamburger patty or a slice of leftover meat loaf.

MAKE THE SANDWICH SPREAD: In a small bowl, combine the Fermented Sweet Pickle Relish, Fermented Mayonnaise, and Fermented Ketchup. Set aside.

MAKE THE SWISS MUSHROOM MELT: In a medium skillet over medium-low heat, melt 2 tablespoons (28 g) of the butter. Sauté the mushrooms for 3 to 4 minutes until cooked through.

Add the Worcestershire sauce, garlic powder, thyme, salt, and pepper and continue cooking the mushrooms until all the liquid has evaporated.

With the remaining butter, butter one side of each slice of bread. Assemble each sandwich, buttered side out, with 1 slice of Swiss, 1 slice of provolone, a generous layer of sautéed mushrooms, and a second slice of Swiss.

In a large skillet over medium-low heat, cook the sandwiches until golden brown and the cheese is melted, about 3 minutes per side.

Remove the sandwiches from the stove and allow to cool slightly. Open each sandwich and add a thin layer of the Sandwich Spread. Serve immediately.

"Everything" Hot Dog Sauce

YIELD: 1½ CUPS (355 ML)

- ½ cup (123 g) Fermented Sweet Pickle Relish (See page 132.)
- 2 tablespoons (22 g) yellow mustard
- 2 tablespoons (30 g) Fermented Ketchup (See page 68.)
- ½ cup (80 g) finely chopped onion

This is the perfect blend of all your favorite hot dog toppings already mixed together. No more lugging multiple bottles of condiments when camping or picnicking! It's great not only on hot dogs, but on brats and burgers too.

In a bowl, combine the Fermented Sweet Pickle Relish, mustard, Fermented Ketchup, and onion. Mix well. Transfer to a jar, cover, and store in the refrigerator for up to 1 month. Serve as a topping for hot dogs or burgers.

 YELLOW MUSTARD

Yellow mustard was first popularized at the St. Louis World's Fair in 1904. It's made from ground mustard seeds, or mustard flour, and mixed with spices and vinegar.

Mustard seed is a source of potassium, which can help maintain healthy heart rhythm and help manage blood pressure. Potassium can also assist with healthy digestion, ensure normal cell function, manage electrolyte balance, and is connected to regulation of electrical signals in the nervous system.

The mustard seed is a real nutrition superstar. It is also a source of phosphorus, which helps the body develop healthy bones and teeth. This mineral is found inside every cell in your body. Like potassium, phosphorus is also connected to a healthy cardiovascular system and healthy blood pressure. Phosphorus can also help your body process B vitamins and help with kidney function, which can rid the body of toxins.

Mustard supplies magnesium, a mineral that helps the release of energy in the body through the ATP cycle. Magnesium is used to maintain the health of many systems in your body.

Crab and Shrimp Louis

- -

FOR THE THOUSAND ISLAND DRESSING:

½ cup (115 g) Fermented Mayonnaise (See page 156.)

¼ cup (61 g) Fermented Sweet Pickle Relish (See page 132.)

¼ cup (60 g) Fermented Ketchup (See page 68.)

FOR THE SALAD:

1 head of romaine lettuce, shredded

½ of an English cucumber, thinly sliced

1 ripe avocado, pitted, peeled, and sliced

2 medium tomatoes, quartered

4 large hard-boiled eggs, peeled and sliced

8 ounces (225 g) lump crabmeat (fresh or canned)

8 ounces (225 g) cooked and peeled wild-caught shrimp

This California original of seafood atop fresh greens is defined, in part, by its creamy Thousand Island Dressing. If you wish, you can use either all shrimp or all crab.

- -

MAKE THE THOUSAND ISLAND DRESSING: Combine the Fermented Mayonnaise, Fermented Sweet Pickle Relish, and Fermented Ketchup. Mix well.

MAKE THE SALADS: Evenly divide the lettuce, cucumber, avocado, tomatoes, eggs, crab, and shrimp among 4 salad plates. Spoon the Thousand Island Dressing over the salad just before serving.

 CUCUMBERS

Cucumbers are a great source of vitamin C. This vitamin protects the body from the damage of free radicals, which are connected to aging and disease. This antioxidant activity can help reduce the risk for cancer and illnesses. Collagen production is aided by vitamin C and it is also known to help your body digest dietary fat.

Vitamin K is also found in cucumbers. This vitamin is helpful in thinning blood and keeping your vascular system running smoothly. When you eat cucumbers, use the peel because it is where half of the vitamin K is found.

Potassium is found in cucumbers as well. This mineral helps your body build and manage muscle tissue. It helps with electrical functioning of your nervous system and can help reduce the risk of high blood pressure, which is connected to stroke risk.

Chapter 10

Sweet and Spicy
Tomato Mango Salsa

Beans, ground squash seeds, and fruit were used in the earliest versions of salsa. Chile peppers and tomatillos or tomatoes were used as well to craft this spicy, tasty condiment. Some experts think it may have been created as far back at the Aztec era around 3000 B.C.E.

Tomatillos are indigenous to the Andes in Peru, Ecuador, and Columbia, and tomatoes are native to Ecuador and Peru. Tomatoes became a staple in salsa once tomato plants became cultivated and widely available. There are several stories about the history of the term "salsa." Some historical sources credit the term to a Spanish priest named Alonso de Molina, who reportedly coined the word in 1571 while others credit the conquistadores. One thing historians agree on, the Spanish people were exposed to the tomato-laden version of salsa in 1521 after conquering the Aztecs.

Modern-day salsa varies from mild to hot and can include onions, lime juice, and cilantro leaves. It's typically served as an accompaniment to Mexican cuisine.

Many people believe that before refrigeration, salsa was most likely fermented as a method of preservation. Introducing beneficial probiotic bacteria into an already delicious and popular condiment is the perfect way to help ensure you get your fermented foods every day.

Sweet and Spicy Tomato Mango Salsa

YIELD: ABOUT 3 CUPS
(780 G)

- -

EQUIPMENT YOU'LL NEED:

Mixing bowls and spoons

*1 glass quart (950 ml) jar
with lid*

*Cheesecloth or cotton
fabric square*

Rubber band or string

INGREDIENTS:

2 jalapenos peppers

*2 cups (360 g) peeled and
chopped tomatoes*

*2 cloves of garlic, minced
or pressed*

*1 cup (175 g) chopped
fresh mango*

*1 tablespoon (6 g) minced
or finely grated fresh
ginger*

*¼ teaspoon ground cumin
and white pepper*

½ teaspoon sea salt

¼ cup (85 g) raw honey

*2 tablespoons (28 ml) raw
apple cider vinegar*

1 teaspoon grated lime zest

Juice of 1 lime

*2 tablespoons (28 ml)
Whey (See page 168.) or
brine from a vegetable
ferment*

The bright color and flavors of this sweet and spicy salsa are a great complement to both grilled and slow-roasted foods. It pairs particularly well with pork and seafood. Due to the sweetness of the mango, this salsa is fermented for a short period (8 to 12 hours), then moved to the refrigerator, which makes it perfect for busy people and those new to fermentation.

- -

Stem, seed, and finely chop the jalapeños. Add them to a bowl and gently combine with the tomatoes, garlic, mango, ginger, cumin, white pepper, and salt. In another bowl, combine the honey, vinegar, lime zest, and lime juice and stir this into the vegetable mixture. Stir in the Whey.

Transfer the mixture to a jar and push down slightly with a spoon to remove any air pockets. Cover the top with cheesecloth or cotton fabric, secured with a rubber band or string. Ferment at room temperature (about 70°F, or 21°C) for 8 to 12 hours.

Cover with an airtight lid and store in the refrigerator overnight for the flavors to combine. Sweet and Spicy Tomato Mango Salsa will keep in the refrigerator for up to 2 weeks.

NOTES: Feel free to adapt this recipe to your personal heat tolerance. If you don't want a lot of spice, reduce the jalapeños to just ½ of a chile; if, after fermenting and chilling, it's still too spicy, add additional honey and mangoes to dilute the heat.

If your home is colder than 68°F (20°C), create a warm fermentation station using the tips on page 17.

Cheesy Scrambled Eggs with Chunky Avocado Salsa

YIELD: 2 SERVINGS

FOR THE CHUNKY AVOCADO SALSA:

1 ripe avocado, pitted, peeled, and chopped

¼ cup (65 g) Sweet and Spicy Tomato Mango Salsa (See page 148.)

1 tablespoon (1 g) chopped fresh cilantro

FOR THE SCRAMBLED EGGS:

4 large eggs

Pinch of sea salt and ground black pepper

1 tablespoon (14 g) butter

½ cup (58 g) shredded pepper Jack or Cheddar cheese

OPTIONAL TOPPINGS:

Crème Fraîche (See page 20.)

Fresh cilantro leaves

Pasture-raised eggs, paired with the healthy fats of avocado, deliver essential nutrients in this tasty and quick meal. No matter how busy your morning is, in less than 10 minutes you can easily transform these ingredients into a healthy start to your day.

MAKE THE CHUNKY AVOCADO SALSA: In a bowl, combine the avocado, Sweet and Spicy Tomato Mango Salsa, and cilantro. Gently stir and set aside.

MAKE THE SCRAMBLED EGGS: In a small bowl, whip the eggs with the salt and pepper.

In a medium skillet over medium heat, melt the butter and then pour in the eggs. Gently stirring continuously, cook until the eggs are set but not dry. Turn off the heat. Top with the shredded cheese and cover with a lid just until the cheese melts.

Serve the eggs topped with the Chunky Avocado Salsa, Crème Fraîche, and cilantro.

 HOW TO MAKE A STAINLESS-STEEL SKILLET NONSTICK

The trick to cooking in a stainless-steel skillet is easy: hot pan/cold fat or hot fat/cold food. It may take you a few tries to find the perfect heat settings on your stove and skillet.

1. Preheat a stainless-steel skillet over medium heat until you can feel the heat when your hand is placed about a 1 inch (2.5 cm) above the pan's surface.
2. Generously add cold fat and reduce the heat to medium-low. Gently swirl the pan to coat the entire surface area. If the butter immediately starts to brown, either the heat is too high or the pan is just a little too hot.
3. Once the fat and the pan are heated, add the room-temperature or cold food. By preheating the pan and then adding the fat, it seals the surface of the skillet so that food is less likely to stick. It's also preferable to treat a stainless-steel skillet similarly to cast iron: Avoid using soap and allow it to become naturally seasoned, washing only with very hot water and an abrasive brush.

Guacamole Dip

YIELD: 4 SERVINGS

----

2 ripe avocados, peeled,
   pitted, and chopped

¼ cup (65 g) Sweet and
   Spicy Tomato Mango
   Salsa (See page 148.)

2 tablespoons (2 g)
   chopped fresh cilantro

Juice of ½ of a lime

Pinch of red pepper
   flakes (optional)

Sea salt, to taste

Tortilla chips, for serving

You probably thought it was impossible to improve upon the
health-boosting deliciousness of guacamole, but the addition
of fermented Sweet and Spicy Tomato Mango Salsa takes it to
a whole new level of yum!

Using a fork, coarsely mash the avocados in a medium bowl. Mix in
the Sweet and Spicy Tomato Mango Salsa, cilantro, lime juice, and
red pepper flakes, if using. Season with the salt. Serve as a dip with
tortilla chips.

✳ LIME

Lime juice can be used in many different recipes to give a
flavor boost, from pie to guacamole to margaritas. Fresh
lime juice is a source of vitamin C, a vitamin important for the
growth and repair of all body tissues and for maintenance of
bones, teeth, and collagen. Collagen helps produce cartilage, ligaments, tendons, and blood vessels.

The compounds in limes known as flavonol glycosides have
antioxidant benefits. Researchers have noted that the flavonoids in citrus fruits such as limes, lemons, and oranges, have
antibiotic properties and might prevent the spread of cancer
cells. Plus they have anti-tumor properties. Many cancer
experts have recommended including at least one serving of
citrus fruit daily to help fight cancer risk.

There are eight different types of compounds found in
limes that promote detoxifying effects in the liver. These
compounds are called liminoids and they help to fight off the
cancer promoting effects of certain chemicals.

Southwest Shrimp and Scallop Ceviche

YIELD: 4 SERVINGS

- *8 ounces (225 g) small peeled wild-caught shrimp*
- *8 ounces (225 g) wild-caught bay scallops*
- *Juice of 4 limes*
- *½ cup (130 g) Sweet and Spicy Tomato Mango Salsa (See page 148.)*
- *¼ cup (40 g) chopped red onion*
- *½ of a jalapeño, finely chopped*
- *¼ cup (4 g) chopped fresh cilantro*
- *1 ripe avocado, pitted, peeled, and chopped*

A staple in Mexican cuisine, ceviche describes raw seafood that "cooked" (marinated) in acidic lime juice. This recipe can be made with any combination of 1 pound (455 g) of fresh, wild-caught seafood, including shrimp, scallops, halibut, red snapper, flounder, and swordfish. If you'd prefer to precook your seafood, refer to the Note below for instructions.

Rinse the shrimp and scallops and place in a medium bowl. Pour the lime juice over top. The seafood should be completely immersed in the lime juice. Refrigerate for 8 to 12 hours until the seafood is opaque.

Discard half of the lime juice from the bowl. Add the Sweet and Spicy Tomato Mango Salsa, red onion, jalapeño, cilantro, and avocado and gently stir. Serve immediately.

NOTE: If you prefer, the seafood can be quickly cooked in boiling water for 2 to 3 minutes until opaque. Do not overcook. Drain well and omit the lime juice soaking. Reduce the limes to 2, mix everything together, and allow to marinate in the refrigerator for 1 hour before serving.

Cowboy Caviar with Tortilla Chips

YIELD: 8 CUPS (1.5 KG)

----

1 can (15 ounces, or
  425 g) black beans,
  drained and rinsed

1 can (15 ounces, or
  425 g) black-eyed peas,
  drained and rinsed

2 cups (325 g) cooked
  corn kernels

½ cup (130 g) Sweet and
  Spicy Tomato Mango
  Salsa (See page 148.)

1 large ripe avocado,
  pitted, peeled,
  and diced

½ of a medium red
  onion, chopped

¼ cup (4 g) chopped
  fresh cilantro

Juice of 1 lime

2 tablespoons (28 ml)
  olive oil

1 teaspoon sea salt

½ teaspoon finely ground
  black pepper

Tortilla chips, for serving

This fresh, healthy, and delicious Cowboy Caviar is elevated by adding fermented salsa to it. Even kids love this. You can make it ahead, so it's great for a summer party. Serve it with scoop-shaped tortilla chips.

In a bowl, combine the black beans, black-eyed peas, corn, Sweet and Spicy Tomato Mango Salsa, avocado, red onion, cilantro, lime juice, olive oil, sea salt, and pepper. Cover and chill until ready to serve. Serve with tortilla chips.

✳ CILANTRO

Cilantro was used by the Greeks during ancient times as a perfume scent and also as an essential oil. The Romans in medieval times used the fresh and fragrant scent to cover up the smell of rotting meat. Natural foods enthusiasts use it today for its pain-relief properties.

Cilantro, which are the leaves of the coriander plant, is often touted for its ability to cleanse the body of toxic metal exposure. Some of the compounds in cilantro bind to and remove toxic metals from the body's tissues. When people suffer from overexposure to mercury, sometimes through excessive intake of seafood, large quantities of cilantro have been shown to reduce symptoms of disorientation.

Consuming cilantro:
» Can help prevent damage to your cardiovascular system
» Adds antioxidants to your diet
» May help fight anxiety symptoms
» Might help lower blood sugar levels, improving side effects from diabetes
» Oil (in coriander seeds) may decrease oxidative stress and damage in the body

Avocado Bruschetta with Pomegranate Molasses

YIELD: 16 PIECES

---

1 baguette, sliced into
    16 slices (½ inch, or
    1.3 cm)

2 tablespoons (28 g)
    butter or ghee, melted

½ cup (60 ml)
    pomegranate juice

1 cup (260 g) Sweet and
    Spicy Tomato Mango
    Salsa (See page 148.),
    drained

2 ripe avocados, pitted,
    peeled, and diced

Sea salt and freshly
    ground black pepper,
    to taste

¼ cup (10 g) fresh basil
    leaves, chopped

If you prefer, use gluten-free bread in place of the baguette. Cut sandwich-style slices of bread into quarters for toast points and bake according to the instructions.

Preheat the oven to 350°F (180°C, or gas mark 4). Line a baking sheet with parchment paper.

Place the baguette slices on the prepared baking sheet. Drizzle with the melted butter. Bake until golden brown, 8 to 10 minutes.

Meanwhile, pour the pomegranate juice into a small saucepan over medium heat. Bring to a slight boil and reduce by half, about 8 to 10 minutes. Set the reduction aside.

In a large bowl, gently toss together the Sweet and Spicy Tomato Mango Salsa and avocados and season with salt and pepper. Top each baguette slice with the tomato mixture and garnish with the basil. Drizzle with the pomegranate reduction and serve immediately.

 POMEGRANATE JUICE

A number of studies have shown that pomegranate juice is linked to health benefits.

Pomegranate juice may help fight breast cancer. The juice has been shown to prevent development of breast cancer cells and may destroy them.

PSA is a blood test measuring a protein connected with prostate cancer. In a study of men who had prostate cancer, 8 ounces (236 ml) of pomegranate juice was shown to keep PSA blood levels stable.

Pomegranate juice may help manage cartilage in your joints preventing deterioration that can lead to osteoarthritis.

Amyloid plaque buildup is connected to Alzheimer's disease risk. One study showed that pomegranate juice may help prevent buildup of amyloid plaque in mice. The study found that the mice that drank the juice were better at performing certain mental tasks.

One study showed that drinking just 1.7 ounces (50 ml) of pomegranate juice is linked to a 5 percent reduction in systolic blood pressure.

Chef's Salad with Creamy Tomato Dressing

YIELD: 4 SERVINGS

FOR THE CREAMY TOMATO DRESSING:

1 medium tomato, cored, peeled, and coarsely chopped

½ cup (115 g) Fermented Mayonnaise (See below.)

2 tablespoons (25 ml) juice from Sweet and Spicy Tomato Mango Salsa (See page 148.)

Sea salt and ground black pepper, to taste

FOR THE CHEF'S SALAD:

3 or 4 heads of romaine lettuce, torn into bite-size pieces (about 8 cups, or 376 g)

1 cup (150 g) each julienned deli ham and turkey

6 scallions, finely chopped

1 cup (150 g) cherry or grape tomatoes, halved

½ cup (58 g) each shredded or julienned Swiss cheese and Cheddar cheese

2 hard-boiled eggs, sliced

4 slices of bacon, cooked and crumbled

Chef's salad is a staple on most restaurant menus. Fermented Mayonnaise updates this classic dish with a boost of probiotic goodness.

MAKE THE CREAMY TOMATO DRESSING: Using a blender, combine the tomato, Fermented Mayonnaise, and Sweet and Spicy Tomato Mango Salsa juice. Blend until smooth, add salt and pepper, and set aside.

   MAKE THE CHEF'S SALAD: Divide the lettuce, ham, turkey, scallions, tomatoes, Swiss, Cheddar, eggs, and bacon among 4 plates or bowls. Serve with a generous drizzle of Creamy Tomato Dressing.

 HOW TO MAKE FERMENTED MAYONNAISE:

For years, mayonnaise has had a bad health rap because of its high fat content, but we now know that not all fats are bad. When mayonnaise is made with pasture-raised eggs and healthy fats (such as olive oil or avocado oil), it is much healthier than its jarred counterparts. Making homemade mayonnaise is the best way to ensure that the ingredients are indeed healthy. If, however, you'd prefer to buy yours, refer to the Resources, page 184. Here's how to make your own:

   In a blender, combine 1 egg yolk, 1 tablespoon (15 ml) Whey (page 168), 1 teaspoon freshly squeezed lemon juice, ¼ teaspoon raw honey, ¼ teaspoon sea salt, and ¼ teaspoon Dijon mustard. Once well combined, with your blender running on low, slowly drizzle in avocado oil (up to 1 cup, or 235 ml). It will emulsify and thicken; keep drizzling oil until your desired thickness is achieved. It will keep, refrigerated, for up to 2 weeks.

Creamy Chilled Gazpacho

YIELD: 6 TO 8 SERVINGS

----

4 cups (950 ml) tomato
    juice

1 cup (260 g) Sweet and
    Spicy Tomato Mango
    Salsa (See page 148.)

3 medium tomatoes,
    peeled and chopped

1 cucumber, peeled,
    seeded, and chopped

1 sweet red or green bell
    pepper, seeded and
    chopped

2 celery stalks, chopped

½ cup (115 g) Crème
    Fraîche (See page 20.),
    plus more for serving
    (optional)

1 tablespoon (4 g)
    chopped fresh flat-leaf
    parsley

1 tablespoon (3 g)
    chopped fresh chives

1 clove of garlic, minced

2 tablespoons (28 ml)
    freshly squeezed
    lemon juice

2 teaspoons raw honey

1 teaspoon Worcestershire
    sauce

Sea salt and ground black
    pepper, to taste

Hot sauce, to taste

A hot day calls for a light, refreshing dish. Gazpacho is just what you need to cool off. This recipe includes savory tomato soup and fresh vegetables with a creamy, fermented twist. Feel free to make this soup as chunky or as smooth as you desire. Traditional gazpacho has some chunks of vegetable, but I often blend mine into a smooth, drinkable chilled soup.

In a blender, combine the tomato juice, Sweet and Spicy Tomato Mango Salsa, tomatoes, cucumber, bell pepper, celery, Crème Fraîche, parsley, chives, garlic, lemon juice, honey, and Worcestershire sauce (you may have to do this in batches). Blend slightly until the desired consistency is reached. Season with salt, black pepper, and hot sauce. Place in a nonreactive storage container, cover tightly, and refrigerate overnight to allow the flavors to blend.

    Serve chilled, with an extra dollop of Crème Fraîche on top, if desired.

✳ TOMATOES

Although tomatoes were once feared as being toxic, they have proven to be one of the most versatile, healthful foods around. They are terrific when stewed or cooked, eliciting a sweet flavor and welcoming aroma, and they are just as easy to chop and eat raw, lending a delicious flavor to sandwiches and salads.

Tomatoes have several health benefits including:

» Helps prevent cancer. The risk for stomach, lung, and prostate cancer is lower in people who eat more servings of tomatoes.

» helps Fight DNA damage. Free radicals can elicit DNA damage. The vitamins A and C in tomatoes help fight this damage from free radicals.

» Helps fight heart disease. Tomatoes are rich in vitamins that help reduce risk for heart disease. These vitamins include B_6, niacin, and folate.

» helps Fend off inflammation. One study found that having a glass of tomato juice every day can lower levels of a compound associated with inflammation called TNF-alpha.

Slow Cooker Pork Tacos with Pineapple Salsa

YIELD: 4 TO 6 SERVINGS

FOR THE PINEAPPLE SALSA:

½ of a pineapple, peeled, cored, and finely diced

1 jalapeño, finely chopped

¼ cup (38 g) finely chopped red bell pepper

4 scallions, thinly sliced

¼ cup (65 g) Sweet and Spicy Tomato Mango Salsa (See page 148.)

2 tablespoons (2 g) chopped fresh cilantro

FOR THE PORK:

1 pork butt roast (2 to 3 pounds, or 905 g to 1.4 kg)

2 teaspoons sea salt

1 teaspoon finely ground black pepper

2 bags of green tea, tea removed from bags

½ of a pineapple (cut into chunks, including the core)

1 jalapeño

½ of a large onion, chopped

2 cloves of garlic, minced or pressed

1 cup (235 ml) water

FOR SERVING:

8 to 12 corn or flour tortillas

Cabbage Apple Carrot Slaw (See page 87.)

The pork mixture is spicy, and the fruit-flavored salsa is the perfect cool sweetness to offset the spiciness. This recipe uses a whole pineapple for this entire recipe—half, with the core, for the pork, and the remaining half, cored and diced, for the Pineapple Salsa.

MAKE THE PINEAPPLE SALSA: In a large bowl, combine the pineapple, jalapeño, bell pepper, scallions, Sweet and Spicy Tomato Mango Salsa, and fresh cilantro. Mix well, and refrigerate for at least 1 hour before serving. The Pineapple Salsa can also be fermented at room temperature for 8 hours while the roast is cooking, following the same process as for the fermented salsa on page 148.

MAKE THE PORK: Season the pork butt with the salt, pepper, and green tea.

In the bottom of a slow cooker, place the pineapple chunks, jalapeño, onion, garlic, and water. Place the seasoned pork roast on top. Cover and cook on low heat for 8 hours.

Remove the pork from the slow cooker, draining off the juices, and place on a cutting board. Discard the pineapple and vegetables remaining in the slow cooker. Using forks, shred the pork.

Heat the tortillas in a dry skillet over medium-low heat. Top each warmed tortilla with shredded Pork, Cabbage Apple Carrot Slaw, and Pineapple Salsa.

NOTE: The pork can also be made in the oven. Bake in a Dutch oven at 350°F (180°C, or gas mark 4) for 4 hours or until the meat is tender and shreds easily.

Spicy Chipotle Mango Shrimp with Succotash

YIELD: 4 SERVINGS

- -

FOR THE SAUCE:

1 mango, peeled, pitted, and coarsely chopped

1 chipotle chile pepper in adobo sauce, plus 1 tablespoon (20 g) adobo sauce (See Note.)

1 tablespoon (15 ml) water

FOR THE SUCCOTASH:

2 tablespoons (28 ml) olive oil, divided

1 small red onion, chopped

½ teaspoon sea salt

¼ teaspoon ground black pepper

1 jalapeño, seeded and minced

1 red bell pepper, finely chopped

2 cups corn kernels, (328 g) frozen or (308 g) fresh cobs

½ cup (78 g) fresh or (80 g) frozen baby lima beans

¼ cup (65 g) Sweet and Spicy Tomato Mango Salsa (See page 148.)

FOR THE SHRIMP:

1 pound (455 g) peeled wild-caught shrimp

When you are craving a lighter, cleaner, but still-filling meal, this is the perfect choice. Cook up corn kernels, lima beans, and chile and bell peppers for a delightful succotash, and pair it with a sinfully spicy shrimp skewer coated with mango adobo sauce!

- -

Place eight 10-inch (20 cm) skewers in a large dish and cover with water. Let stand for 15 minutes.

MAKE THE SAUCE: Meanwhile, in a food processor, pulse the mango, chipotle chile, adobo sauce, and water until smooth. Set the sauce aside.

Preheat a grill to medium-high.

MAKE THE SUCCOTASH: In a large skillet, heat 1 tablespoon (15 ml) of the oil over medium-high heat. Add the onion, salt, and pepper and cook for 2 minutes, stirring frequently. Add the jalapeño and red bell pepper and cook for 2 minutes longer, stirring occasionally.

Stir in the corn and lima beans. Cook until all the vegetables are tender-crisp, about 3 to 4 minutes. Remove from the heat and cover to keep warm.

MAKE THE SHRIMP: Divide the shrimp evenly between the eight skewers. Brush the shrimp with the remaining 1 tablespoon (15 ml) oil. Place the shrimp skewers on the hot grill and cook until the shrimp turn opaque throughout, turning once, about 5 to 6 minutes. Remove from the grill and brush with the Mango-Chipotle Sauce.

Toss the Sweet and Spicy Tomato Mango Salsa into the warm succotash and serve with the shrimp skewers.

VARIATIONS

Use 2 boneless, skinless chicken breasts, cut into 1-inch (2.5 cm) pieces, in place of the shrimp.

Use frozen edamame in place of the lima beans, if desired.

NOTE: Chipotles in adobo sauce are sold in small cans in the Latin section of most grocery stores. They tend to be very spicy. For a milder version of this recipe, omit the chipotle chile and use just 1 tablespoon (15 ml) of the adobo sauce. To avoid wasting the rest of the contents of the can, puree the remaining chipotles and sauce and freeze in small ice cube trays for convenient portions to use later.

✳ LIMA BEANS

Lima beans have a velvety texture that may be the inspiration for its nickname, butter beans. They are thought to have gained popularity in Lima, Peru. These beans have many health benefits:

They are rich in soluble fiber, which absorbs water during digestion in the stomach. This action slows the absorption of sugar into the bloodstream, which can help keep blood sugar levels steady.

Lima beans also contain insoluble fiber, which has a scraping action in the digestive tract and also bulks up stool.

They are rich in both calcium and manganese, which help promote strong bones and prevent osteoporosis.

Chapter 11

Yogurt

When probiotic bacteria, also known as yogurt cultures, are mixed with milk, yogurt is formed. The fermentation process acts directly on lactose, a milk sugar, and the bacteria help produce lactic acid. This acid is responsible for the tangy flavor of yogurt. Yogurt is made throughout the world using different types of milk, including that of goats, sheep, camels, yaks, water buffalo, and horses.

There are many benefits to making your own yogurt:

» When yogurt is made commercially, the fermentation process is shorter. This creates a sweet-tasting yogurt. Some of the lactose remains in the product since it's not used up by the bacteria. When yogurt is fermented for a longer period of time, the yogurt produced is lactose-free.

» Making yogurt at home is relatively cheap to do. Commercially prepared yogurt costs more, so homemade yogurt saves money.

» You can control what goes into your yogurt, so you know it's free of additives such as carrageenan, artificial sweeteners, dried milk, or guar gum.

» Because homemade yogurt ferments for longer periods of time, it supplies more probiotic bacteria than commercially prepared yogurt.

» Making yogurt at home is very easy to do. Simply mix the ingredients together, allow them to sit and ferment for 8 to 24 hours, and then enjoy.

» When you make yogurt at home, you can create your own original flavors. You can also control the sweetness or tartness by adjusting the fermentation time.

Yogurt

YIELD: 4 CUPS (920 G)

EQUIPMENT YOU'LL NEED:

Large stainless-steel pot

Instant-read thermometer

Measuring cup

Mixing spoon

1 quart (950 ml) glass jar, 2 pint (475 ml) jars, 4 half-pint (235 ml) jars (canning jars work perfectly), or the jars that came with your yogurt maker with lids

Yogurt maker or other way to incubate the yogurt (See directions for other options.)

INGREDIENTS:

4 cups (946 ml) whole milk (not ultra-pasteurized)

¼ cup (60 g) plain yogurt with live cultures and no other additives (store-bought or saved from a previous batch of homemade) or packaged yogurt starter

There are some beneficial bacteria in store-bought yogurt, but I argue it's not the best choice for your health or your budget! Instead, make your own—it's easy and better for you.

PREPARE THE MILK AND STARTER: In a large pot over medium heat, bring the milk to 185°F (85°C). Remove the pot from the stove.

Let the milk cool to 110°F (43°C), about 20 to 30 minutes. Alternatively, carefully place the pot in a sink full of ice water to speed the cooling process. Once it's cooled, combine ¼ cup (60 ml) of the milk with the plain yogurt starter. Adding the milk before it's cooled may kill the yogurt cultures, so be sure it has cooled enough.

Pour the milk-starter mixture back into the pot and stir. Transfer the mixture to jars, as desired, and seal with the lids.

INCUBATE: Incubate the yogurt in a warm place for 8 to 24 hours until the desired tangy taste is achieved. Choose a place that's out of the way so your yogurt won't be disturbed. While there are many ways to incubate yogurt (see below), the common theme is maintaining a consistent temperature of 100° to 110°F (38° to 43°C) for the entire incubation period. Some methods work better than others, but all can be used. If there is not a thermostat-controlled heat source, check periodically that the temperature is still warm enough during incubation.

COOLER METHOD: Place lidded jars filled with the milk-starter mixture into a small hard-sided cooler. Fill the cooler with hot tap water, just to the bottoms of the lids. Lock the lid in place and, for good measure, wrap the cooler in a large bath towel.

YOGURT MAKER: Yogurt makers, such as the one opposite, are easy to use and are designed specifically for keeping your yogurt at the perfect temperature. Transfer the cooled milk-starter mixture into the jars that came with your maker and place them inside the yogurt maker (consult the instruction manual for details).

FOOD DEHYDRATOR: Yogurt can be incubated in food dehydrators that have adjustable thermostats and enough room to hold the jars. Place lidded jars of milk-starter mixture inside the dehydrator, close the door, and set the temperature at 100° to 110°F (38° to 43°C).

SLOW COOKER: Place lidded jars filled with the milk-starter mixture in a slow cooker and fill the cooker with hot tap water just to the bottoms of the lids. Cover and incubate the yogurt on the warm setting.

OVEN METHOD: Preheat the oven to 110°F (43°C). When it reaches that temperature, turn it off, place your lidded jars filled with milk-starter mixture inside, turn on the oven light, and close the door. (The light will help keep the oven warm.)

Chill the finished yogurt in the refrigerator for at least 2 to 3 hours prior to eating.

NOTE: If you like, you can add sweetener, such as honey; chopped fruit; or flavorings, such as vanilla, to your finished yogurt. If you're using a yogurt starter, it will come with instructions that will tell you when and how to add it to the milk.

 HOW TO MAKE GREEK YOGURT (AND WHEY!)

Refrigerate homemade yogurt for at least 3 hours to allow it to completely cool and thicken. From there, you can make Greek yogurt, using a Greek yogurt strainer or a large strainer lined with four layers of damp cheesecloth set on top of a bowl.

Greek Yogurt: Gently scoop the yogurt into the Greek yogurt maker or cheesecloth-lined strainer—do not dump it, as the force can push yogurt through the fine mesh. Refrigerate overnight (8 to 24 hours) or until the desired consistency is achieved.

Whey: The liquid that has accumulated in the bottom of the bowl is the whey. Store the whey in the refrigerator for months. Use it for lacto-fermenting other foods in this book (such as Sweet and Spicy Tomato Mango Salsa on page 148, Fermented Sweet Pickle Relish on page 132, Fermented Ginger Orange Carrots on page 82, and Dried Fruit Chutney on page 52). Transfer the strained Greek Yogurt to a container with a lid; it will keep in the refrigerator for up to 1 week.

Mocha Banana Breakfast Smoothie

YIELD: 2 SERVINGS

- -

1 cup (80 g) old-fashioned
*   rolled oats*

1 cup (235 ml) milk

1 banana

1 cup (230 g) plain Yogurt
*   (See page 166.)*

1½ tablespoons (8 g)
*   unsweetened cocoa*
*   powder*

1 tablespoon (6 g)
*   espresso powder*

1 cup (118 g) ice cubes

Coffee and breakfast in one blended drink: What could be better on a hectic morning? With just a little prep work the night before and a quick blend in the morning, you'll be off and running in no time!

- -

In a small bowl or jar, stir together the oats and milk. Cover and refrigerate overnight.

The next morning, in a blender, combine the oat mixture, banana, Yogurt, cocoa powder, and espresso powder and blend until smooth.

Add the ice and blend until frothy. Serve immediately.

VARIATIONS:

» Use your choice of nondairy milk in place of the cow's milk.

» Freeze brewed coffee in ice cube trays and use them in place of the espresso powder and ice cubes.

» For a grain-free version, use 1 cup (225 g) cooked sweet potatoes in place of the oats (don't soak the potatoes overnight).

✳ COCOA POWDER

Some studies show that cocoa powder may boost endorphins, which are natural opiates in our system. Endorphins are responsible for happy feelings after laughing or exercise. Cocoa powder may also boost serotonin, which is a brain neurotransmitter connected to happiness. Serotonin is the target of antidepressant medications.

Cocoa powder is also rich in flavonoids, which are part of a group of antioxidants called polyphenols. Studies report that cocoa may be one of the most polyphenol-rich foods available, and drinking hot cocoa may help fight aging, heart disease, and cancer. But don't rely on just any packaged hot cocoa mix to get the full antioxidant benefits. Consider getting raw cocoa powder (also called raw cacao powder), which contains the beneficial compounds.

Strawberry Banana Yogurt To-Go Tubes

YIELD: 6 SERVINGS

----

1 tablespoon (7 g)
    powdered gelatin

2 tablespoons (28 ml)
    warm water

1½ cups (345 g) plain
    Yogurt or Greek Yogurt
    (See pages 166 to 168.)

1 cup (145 g) chopped
    fresh strawberries

1 banana

6 yogurt tubes (See the
    Resources on page 184.)

Your kids can still have supercool, portable yogurts for their lunch, only healthier and more budget friendly by making them yourself. You have the choice of using disposable plastic zip-top bags or silicone molds made specifically for these sweet treats. (See the Resources section, page 184.)

In a small bowl, dissolve the gelatin in the warm water.

In a blender, combine the Yogurt, strawberries, banana, and dissolved gelatin and blend until smooth.

Using a funnel, fill each yogurt tube and seal. Place in the freezer until ready to place in lunch boxes.

VARIATIONS:

Substitute 2 cups (approximately 300 g) of any desired fruit in place of the strawberries and banana.

For a sweeter treat, add honey, maple syrup, or stevia to taste.

✳ GELATIN

Gelatin is a powdered source of protein made from the connective tissue and bones of animals. It doesn't have much flavor. The powder dissolves in hot water or other liquids, and as it cools, it hardens. It contains half of the 18 essential amino acids. Gelatin:

» has 6 g of protein per 1 tablespoon (10 g) serving
» binds to water and helps to move food through the digestive tract, improving digestion
» can help seal off perforations in the stomach and heal the digestive tract and may help with food intolerance
» is rich in amino acids that can help prevent degeneration of joint cartilage, improve joint and bone health, and may have anti-inflammatory properties, which can temper the pain of arthritis
» may improve skin elasticity by encouraging the production of collagen
» is rich in glycine, which can fight inflammation, and may help promote the healing of wounds
» may improve sleep quality, according to studies
» may help keep you alert and aware during the day
» is nutrient-rich and can help with satiety, plus it may promote weight loss

Pesto Buttermilk Ranch Dip and Dressing

- ⅓ cup (75 g) Fermented Mayonnaise (See page 156.)
- ⅓ cup (77 g) Greek Yogurt (See page 168.)
- 2 tablespoons (28 ml) cultured buttermilk or sour cream
- 2 tablespoons (30 g) prepared basil pesto
- 1 tablespoon (4 g) finely chopped fresh flat-leaf parsley or 1 teaspoon dried
- 1 tablespoon (3 g) finely chopped fresh chives or 1 teaspoon dried
- ½ teaspoon finely chopped fresh dill or ⅛ teaspoon dried
- ½ teaspoon raw apple cider vinegar

The zesty combination of pesto and buttermilk ranch makes this probiotic-spiked dip and dressing not just sneakily healthy but also delicious. Freeze leftover pesto in ice cube trays to thaw and use later!

In a bowl, combine the Fermented Mayonnaise, Yogurt, buttermilk, pesto, parsley, chives, dill, and vinegar. Mix well. Refrigerate for at least 1 hour to allow the flavors to combine before serving.

Serve with vegetable crudités as a dip, over a salad as a dressing, or on a sandwich as a spread.

NOTE: If a thinner consistency is desired, add milk or water, 1 tablespoon (28 ml) at a time.

Sweet and Sour Broccoli Slaw

FOR THE DRESSING:

¼ cup (60 g) Fermented
  Mayonnaise (See page
  156.)

¼ cup (60 g) plain Yogurt
  (See page 166.)

3 tablespoons (60 g)
  raw honey

2 tablespoons (28 ml) raw
  apple cider vinegar

Sea salt and ground black
  pepper, to taste

FOR THE SLAW:

3 cups (210 g) shredded
  or coarsely chopped
  broccoli

3 cups (300 g) shredded
  or coarsely chopped
  cauliflower

1 carrot, peeled
  and shredded

¼ cup (40 g) chopped
  red onion

¼ cup (30 g)
  unsweetened dried
  cranberries

4 slices of bacon, cooked
  and crumbled

2 tablespoons (18 g) raw
  unsalted sunflower
  seeds

This crisp, cool salad is a mixture of sweet and sour tastes. It is a refreshing starter dish. If you don't have any yogurt on hand, try it with Crème Fraîche (page 20) instead.

MAKE THE DRESSING: In a small bowl, combine the Fermented Mayonnaise, Yogurt, honey, and vinegar. Mix well and then season with sea salt and black pepper.

MAKE THE SLAW: In a large bowl, combine the broccoli, cauliflower, carrot, onion, cranberries, bacon, and sunflower seeds. Toss with the dressing.

Refrigerate the dressed slaw for at least 1 hour to allow the flavors to combine before serving.

✳ SUNFLOWER SEEDS

Many people love the nutty, savory taste of sunflower seeds. Mix them into prepared pasta and rice dishes or sprinkle them on cereal and in stir-fry dishes. You can stir them into yogurt or add them to a sandwich for a satisfying crunch. There are many ways to add them into the foods you eat. Sunflower seeds also:

» are rich in selenium, which is helpful for fighting cancer
» are a source of copper and magnesium, which promote bone health, and vitamin E, which may ease the pain of arthritis
» may help prevent LDL cholesterol from adhering to artery walls

Smoked Salmon Spread

YIELD: 1½ CUPS (340 G)

----

4 ounces (115 g) cream
cheese, softened

¼ cup (60 g) Crème
Fraîche (See page 20.)

½ cup (115 g) Greek
Yogurt (See page 168.)

Juice of ½ of a lemon

1 tablespoon (4 g)
chopped fresh dill or
1 teaspoon dried

1 tablespoon (15 g)
Dijon mustard

2 teaspoons
Worcestershire sauce

2 scallions, thinly sliced

4 ounces (115 g) wild-
caught smoked salmon,
coarsely chopped

Smoked salmon mixed into a probiotic-rich blend of cream cheese, Crème Fraîche, and Greek yogurt, along with fresh herbs, makes a delicious spread you'll be sure to enjoy.

Using an electric mixer, beat the cream cheese until smooth. Add the Crème Fraîche, Greek Yogurt, lemon juice, dill, mustard, and Worcestershire sauce, continuing to beat until well incorporated.

Gently fold in the scallions and smoked salmon.

Refrigerate for 8 hours to allow the flavors to combine before serving.

Serve in hollowed-out cucumber spears as an appetizer, with crackers as a snack, or spread on a bagel for breakfast.

 WILD-CAUGHT VERSUS FARMED SEAFOOD

Whether you choose shrimp, sea bass, cod, or salmon, know that fish and shellfish are nutritious. Fish is rich in omega-3 fatty acids and many other nutrients and high in protein. Consider the source of the fish you eat, otherwise you may be consuming harmful compounds.

Fish that are farm-raised in controlled enclosures are often exposed to poor conditions and a poor food supply. The feed for the fish may include GMOs and the fish may have higher levels of toxin exposure, disease, and exposure to artificial dyes and antibiotics than wild-caught fish. Fish caught in the wild tend to be higher in omega-3 fatty acids and even higher in protein. Wild fish also have a lower incidence of disease and typically are not exposed to artificial compounds.

Mercury is an issue with some types of fish primarily due to the type of fish that the fish consume. Certain types of fish consume bottom feeder fish, smaller fish that build up more contaminants than other fish. This type of feeding produces higher levels of mercury in larger fish. Mercury is an issue with both farm-raised and wild-caught fish that consume feeder fish. Fish that have higher levels of mercury include swordfish, shark, king mackerel, and tilefish caught in the Gulf of Mexico.

Lamb Kofta with Herbed Tzatziki

YIELD: 4 SERVINGS

FOR THE HERBED TZATZIKI:

1 medium English cucumber

1 cup (230 g) Greek Yogurt (See page 168.)

1 clove of garlic, minced or pressed

Juice of ½ of a lemon

½ teaspoon dried dill weed

Sea salt and ground black pepper, to taste

FOR THE KOFTA:

2 tablespoons (28 g) butter or ghee

1 medium onion, finely chopped

2 cloves of garlic, crushed

1 pound (455 g) ground lamb

2 tablespoons (8 g) chopped fresh flat-leaf parsley or 1 teaspoon dried

(continued on next page)

Kofta is an updated, spicy variation of meatloaf. Ground lamb, dill, and parsley are used as the flavorful base for this unique dish. Served with lots of tzatziki sauce, they'll become a fast favorite of your whole family!

MAKE THE HERBED TZATZIKI: Peel and seed the cucumber, and then grate it. Drain and squeeze, using your hands, to remove the excess water from the grated cucumber (you will have ½ to 1 cup [120 to 240 g] of drained grated cucumber). In a medium bowl, combine the cucumber, Yogurt, garlic, lemon juice, and dill. Season with salt and pepper. Chill in the refrigerator until ready to serve.

Preheat the oven to 350°F (180°C, or gas mark 4).

MAKE THE KOFTA: In a medium skillet, melt the butter over medium heat. Sauté the onion and garlic in the butter until soft and translucent, about 5 to 7 minutes.

In a large bowl, combine the lamb, parsley, mint, oregano, cumin, salt, pepper, cinnamon, nutmeg, and cloves. Add the cooked onion and garlic, then add the egg, and mix well.

Divide the lamb mixture into 8 equal portions, form into oval-shaped meatballs, and place on a sheet of waxed paper.

Heat the oil in a large skillet and brown the koftas for 2 minutes per side. (I like to serve my koftas on kebab sticks, so at this point I skewer them onto bamboo skewers.)

Place on a baking sheet and bake for 10 to 15 minutes until cooked through. (The internal temperature should be 160°F, or 71°C.) Serve the koftas with the Herbed Tzatziki.

VARIATION:

Use ground beef in place of the lamb.

2 tablespoons (12 g) chopped fresh mint or 1 teaspoon dried

1 tablespoon (4 g) chopped fresh oregano or 1 teaspoon dried

2 teaspoons ground cumin

½ teaspoon sea salt

¼ teaspoon ground black pepper

⅛ teaspoon ground cinnamon

⅛ teaspoon ground nutmeg

⅛ teaspoon ground cloves

1 large egg

2 tablespoons (28 g) coconut oil

Frozen Yogurt Bark

YIELD: 4 SERVINGS

----

1 cup (230 g) Greek
   Yogurt (See page 168.)

2 tablespoons (40 g)
   raw honey

2 tablespoons (15 g)
   unsweetened dried
   cranberries

2 tablespoons (18 g)
   raisins

5 fresh strawberries,
   chopped

2 tablespoons (22 g) dark
   chocolate chips

2 tablespoons
   (10 g) flaked dried
   unsweetened coconut

This Frozen Yogurt Bark is made with probiotic-packed Greek Yogurt mixed with honey and covered with sweet strawberries, chewy coconut, and polyphenol-rich dark chocolate chips.

In a medium bowl, mix the yogurt and honey until well combined. Add the cranberries and raisins and stir again.

Line a baking sheet with aluminum foil and pour the yogurt mixture on top. Spread it about ½ inch (1.2 cm) thick.

Sprinkle the strawberries, chocolate chips, and flaked coconut on top and place the baking sheet in the freezer for 1 hour or until it is completely frozen.

Remove from the freezer and use a sharp knife to break the bark into pieces. Store the bark in an airtight container in the freezer for up to 1 month.

 DRIED CRANBERRIES

Cranberries might be small, but they are packed with nutrition. They are often associated with urinary tract health, but they have many more health benefits. In 2009, a study was published in *Health Studies Journal* that found cranberries helped regulate blood sugar levels in individuals with type 2 diabetes. They are also rich in antioxidants that can help manage inflammation and ultimately reduce your risk from cancer and heart disease. If choosing dried cranberries, look for unsweetened or reduced sugar varieties.

Flourless Brownie Bites with Peanut Butter Frosting

YIELD: 16 BROWNIE BITES

FOR THE BROWNIES:

5 Medjool dates, pitted

1 ripe avocado, pitted
   and peeled

½ cup (130 g) natural
   peanut butter

½ cup (40 g)
   unsweetened cocoa
   powder

¼ cup (60 ml) milk

FOR THE FROSTING:

½ cup (130 g) natural
   peanut butter

½ cup (115 g) Greek
   Yogurt (See page 168.)

2 tablespoons (40 g)
   raw honey

Just when you thought chocolate and peanut butter couldn't get any better, I've turned them into a grain- and gluten-free probiotic treat! No one will guess that in addition to the fermented frosting, these are packed with healthy fats from the avocado.

Preheat the oven to 350°F (180°C, or gas mark 4). Grease a mini muffin pan.

MAKE THE BROWNIES: In a food processor, process the dates until well chopped. Add the avocado and process until combined. Add the peanut butter, cocoa powder, and milk and process to blend. Spoon the batter into the muffin cups.

Bake for 15 minutes or until a toothpick in the center comes out clean. Let the brownies cool before removing them from the muffin pan.

MAKE THE FROSTING: In a food processor, combine the peanut butter, Greek Yogurt, and honey and process until creamy.

Frost the cooled brownies. Store the brownie bites in an airtight container in the refrigerator for up to 1 week.

VARIATIONS

For a dairy-free version, substitute coconut or almond milk in place of the dairy milk. For a peanut-free version, substitute almond butter for the peanut butter.

 AVOCADO

Avocado is high in fat, but don't let that stop you from eating it! After all, your brain is made up from 60 percent fat, so you need healthful fats such as avocado in your diet. When fat is included in a meal, your brain gets a signal of fullness, so eating fat can actually help you feel fuller and could lead to weight loss. Fat also slows down the breakdown of dietary carbohydrate, which can help stabilize your blood sugar levels.

Mango Lassi Ice Pops

YIELD: 4 TO 6 POPS

- -

2 mangoes, peeled and
  chopped

1 cup (230 g) plain
  Yogurt, divided (See
  page 166.)

¼ cup (85 g) raw
  honey, divided

Pinch of ground
  cardamom

½ teaspoon vanilla
  extract

Made with creamy yogurt, sweet mango with a pinch of spice,
these Mango Lassi Ice Pops are a decadent dessert for any day of
the year.

- -

In a blender, blend the mangoes with ⅓ cup (77 g) of the Yogurt,
2 tablespoons (40 g) of the honey, and the cardamom until smooth.

In a separate bowl, combine the remaining ⅔ cup (153 g) yogurt,
remaining 2 tablespoons (40 g) honey, and vanilla.

Alternate layering the mango puree and the yogurt mixture into ice
pop molds. Freeze for 6 to 8 hours until completely frozen.

Chapter 12

Troubleshooting
and Resources

Troubleshooting

It's easy to prepare fermented foods in your own kitchen, and if you closely follow guidelines and directions, there are usually no problems. Because you're dealing with live probiotic bacteria, be sure to handle the bacteria properly to avoid issues.

With guidance, these difficulties can be minimized. They can occur if the right temperature isn't maintained (watch that the temperature is not too high). Monitor how much contact the ferments have with air. Common problems can arise when vegetables are not fully submerged in the liquid. Also, be sure that your hands, utensils, storage containers, and foods are all clean. Here are the ways that ferments can go awry because of any (or all) of these problems:

Soft and mushy vegetables: If you maintain the proper temperature during fermentation you can avoid this occurrence. Although these vegetables are still fine to eat, they lose some of their crunchiness.

Very dark-colored vegetables: With fermentation, it's common for the color of the vegetables to change; however, very darkly colored vegetables should be discarded. Color change can be due to the presence of contaminants during fermentation. For example, salt should be distributed evenly and if it's not, undesirable organisms can overtake the ferment. Another reason is an inadequate level of juice, which allows some yeasts and bacteria to flourish on the surfaces of the vegetables that are left uncovered. Finally, too high a temperature during fermentation may encourage the growth of undesirable bacteria, which leads to unappetizing, dark coloration.

Pink sauerkraut, or when non-red vegetables turn pink: There is a group of yeasts that often produce red pigmentation on the surface of cabbage and in the juice. When yeasts multiply, this is typically because of an uneven distribution of, or too much, salt. If you create conditions optimal for normal fermentation, these spoilage yeasts are suppressed. If your vegetables turn pink, but they are supposed to be green, you may not find them appetizing enough to eat.

When using red cabbage or other red vegetables, the color can sometimes fade to a pinkish color, but this is not a sign of problems or spoilage.

A white or colorful coating on the surface: Sometimes a white-colored coating that floats on the surface is a type of yeast called *kahm*. This is not desirable and can develop as the pH level drops in the ferment and the lactic acid bacteria eat up all of the sugar. One sign that your ferment has developed kahm yeast is that the white coating develops thin hair-like strands. When you see this, simply skim it off the ferment and discard it. The vegetables should still be fine. One of the reasons that the kahm yeast develops is because the vegetables are not fully submerged in the liquid and have been exposed to air. Also, be sure that the room temperature does not exceed 72°F (22°C).

A colorful coating of mold on the surface: If the temperature is too high, or the vegetables are not fully submerged in the liquid, they may develop a colorful coating. In some cases, an excess of salt is used in the ferment, preventing adequate lactic acid production. Sometimes this can be caused by organisms or bacteria on the vegetables before being cultured. Also, organisms could be introduced through contamination of the equipment.

The brine is foamy: Certain types of foods have a high sugar content, which provides lots of food for the bacteria to quickly consume, often resulting in foam forming on top of the brine. Some foods that are higher in sugar include apples, carrots, and beets. Sometimes bubbles form in the ferment as well. Foam and bubbles in your ferment are completely normal and a result of the probiotic bacterial action at work.

Powerful odor: Good bacteria work to utilize sugar and transform it into gas and acid. This is completely normal. It can cause a strong odor but it should not smell rotten or moldy, which could indicate a problem. The temperature of the room shouldn't exceed 72°F (22°C). Be sure that your utensils, containers, and hands are clean before you start working. Don't consume any ferments that have a bad smell.

The brine is slimy: Some microorganisms produce slime, which can produce a slimy ferment. Keep the temperature stable and use enough brine to cover the vegetables to avoid this.

Excessively salty taste: When you don't use a starter culture, you can run the risk of a salty product. Also, adding too much salt can change the sequence of the bacterial fermentation and produce a salty taste. If you do add too much salt by mistake, try diluting it with additional liquid, such as celery or cabbage juice.

Another way to dilute the saltiness is to use water that has been boiled (to kill bacteria) and cooled. When you do use a starter culture, and this is absolutely the best way to ferment, you won't need to add any salt. Use the best quality starter culture, and if you want to add salt, use a minimal amount.

Leaky jars: It is completely normal for the brine to bubble and leak from the jar lid. This shows that the good bacteria are hard at work! One way to manage leaky jars is to leave some space between the top of the brine and the jar lid, thereby allowing room for the brine to bubble up and expand. A good rule to follow is to fill the jar about 80 percent full. Don't tighten the lids completely since this will allow some gas to escape.

White yeasty sediment: Some of the yeast may settle on the bottom of the jars. You can eat the vegetables as long as they look and smell good. Don't eat them if they are moldy or have a slimy texture.

Brine is cloudy: A cloudy brine is normal. This is caused by the lactic acid created during fermentation, and this lactic acid also lends a tangy taste to vegetables and is quite healthful!

Faded and dull-colored vegetables: Although we may be used to identifying healthy vegetables by their bright color, it's normal for the color to fade during fermentation. Even the most brightly colored vegetables will fade. In fact, this is a sign that the fermentation process is successful. The fading is caused by the bacteria acting on the sugars and the pigments in the vegetables, and is a normal part of the process.

Resources

✳ *Fermentation Cultures, Starters, and Supplies* ✳

Kombucha Shop
Kombucha SCOBYs, kombucha starter kits, and kombucha supplies such as pH testing strips
www.thekombuchashop.com

Cultures for Health
Vegetable starter, crème fraîche, and yogurt starters
www.culturesforhealth.com

New England Cheesemaking Supply Co.
Crème fraîche and yogurt starters
www.cheesemaking.com

Amazon
When in doubt, look on Amazon! They have jars, bottles, kefir grains, kombucha SCOBYs, and miscellaneous fermentation equipment (pickle pebbles, pH testing strips, silicone yogurt tubes, pounders, airlocks, and more).
www.amazon.com

Craigslist
Look here for used canning jars and antique fermentation supplies. Individuals, like me, will also list their extra kefir grains and kombucha SCOBYs.
www.craigslist.com

Weck Jars
The French-style jars shown in most of the photos in this book
www.weckjars.com

Ball Mason Canning Jars
Wide-mouth canning jars and lids
www.freshpreserving.com

Anchor Hocking

Jars and bottles (specifically, the 1-gallon [3.8 L] canister jar used for kombucha)
www.oneida.com

Facebook

Join our group for fermentation fun, support, and starter exchanging.
www.facebook.com/groups/fermentedfoodsateverymeal/

✳ *Miscellaneous Supplies and Ingredients* ✳

Coconut Secret

Coconut Aminos Soy-free alternative to soy sauce
www.coconutsecret.com

Lodge Cast Iron

Cast-iron skillets
www.lodgemfg.com

Euro Cuisine

Greek Yogurt Maker
www.eurocuisine.net

hydrofarm

Seedling Heat Mat and Thermostat
www.hydrofarm.com

Nor Pro

BPA-Free Popsicle Molds
www.norpro.com

Vital Proteins

Collagen Peptides and Powdered Gelatin
www.vitalproteins.com

About the Author

Hayley Barisa Ryczek is the voice behind the healthy cooking and natural lifestyle blog *Health Starts in the Kitchen*. After a diagnosis of celiac disease in 2010, Hayley eliminated grains and gluten from her diet and set up a blog to help others enjoy a traditional real-foods diet, including fermented foods.

Hayley's recipes have been featured in *Reader's Digest, Wellness* magazine, and on the websites of David Perlmutter, M.D., and Paleo Parents. She has also written *Grain-Free Grab-n-Go*, a snack cookbook, and cowritten another recipe book, *Make it Paleo II*. Her blog has earned her recognition in the Paleohacks Awards 2015 and the Mamavation Top Green & Wellness Blogs of 2014.

Index